1695

UNDER THE

Canopy

GFWC TALLAHASSEE JUNIOR WOMAN'S CLUB, INC.
TALLAHASSEE, FLORIDA

Printed in the USA by

WIMMER
The Wimmer Companies, Inc.
Memphis • Dallas

UNDER THE CANOPY COMMITTEES

Donna Peacock
Chairman

Margaret Rodrigue
Co-Chairman

Candy Mitchell
Co-Chairman

Executive Steering Committee
Candi Aubin
Sally Baker
Kathleen Brennan
Shari Cromar
Susan Harrell-Swartz
Janyce Horton
Jan James
Annette Marshall
D.J. Matthias
Pat Thomas

Food Editors

Mary Brown
Jennifer Craig
Beth Hamilton

Carol Lanfri
Brunetta Pfaender
Nona Yaw

Proofing and Editing
Diane Mann

Typesetting/Layout
Dianne Brantly

Interior Art
Anne Kozeliski

Forward
Mary Ann Lindley

Marketing
Tommie Cochran

Dedication

The GFWC Tallahassee Junior Woman's Club of Tallahassee, Florida expresses its grateful appreciation to its members and friends who have contributed their recipes, time and efforts, all of which have made this book possible.

Thank You

The GFWC Tallahassee Junior Woman's Club of Tallahassee, Florida would like to thank the Historic Tallahassee Preservation Board for their assistance in research on the sites in this publication.

The Woman's Club of Tallahassee

The Woman's Club of Tallahassee clubhouse is a one story Mediterranean Revival structure, built of concrete block and finished with textured stucco. The roof is a low hip covered with pantile tiles. It is surrounded on three sides by several large old live oak trees hung with Spanish moss which create a protective canopy over the clubhouse.

The Woman's Club of Tallahassee was organized in 1903 with the primary goals of unity, liberty, charity, generosity, health, and hope. With such aspirations and a spirit of volunteerism, the Woman's Club has been the catalyst for the improvement of the community through its many projects. These projects have included the planting and protection of Tallahassee's magnificent trees, the establishment of Leon High School, and historical preservation and restoration of the Union Bank Building and the Old Capitol. In addition, its many humanitarian projects focusing on children, family, health, and welfare issues have continually demonstrated its spirit of generosity and commitment to community improvement.

Since its dedication on April 19, 1927, the Clubhouse in Los Robles, Tallahassee's first prestigious suburb, has been used as a civic and entertainment center. From community meetings to dances, banquets, wedding receptions, and other parties, the Clubhouse has been a prominent part of Tallahassee's social life. The Clubhouse is listed on the National Register of Historic Places.

The GFWC Tallahassee Junior Woman's Club wishes to thank the Woman's Club of Tallahassee for their constant encouragement and friendship.

TABLE OF CONTENTS

APPETIZERS & BEVERAGES 15

SOUPS & SALADS 43

BREADS 67

CHEESE & EGGS 85

ENTRÉES 97
   (MEAT (BEEF, LAMB, PORK), POULTRY, GAME,
   SEAFOOD , VEGETARIAN)

PASTA & RICE 173

VEGETABLES 201

ACCOMPANIMENTS 229
   (STUFFING, SAUCES, FRUIT)

DESSERTS 247
   (CAKES , CANDY, COOKIES & BARS, PIES)

EQUIVALENT MEASURES 295

INDEX 299

Canopy Roads

Gracious old live oak trees reach across the road, creating the effect of a canopy. Grey and ghostly Spanish moss drips from the trees, adding a mystical effect. Small saplings and vines weave in and out of the live oaks, completing the enclosed canopy.

PREFACE

As the 20th Century draws to a close, possibly the most direct way to find the heart of Tallahassee is to travel outward from it -- out beyond the city limits along its five famous canopy roads, beneath the leafy ceilings of Centerville, Miccosukee, Meridian, St. Augustine and Old Bainbridge roads to where open countryside is quickly found.

Tallahassee has enjoyed the amenities of growth, which has shot our countryside population beyond 200,000 in too few years for oldtimers and natives to quite fathom.

Along with the rest of Florida, we've endured some impudent gestures of man as well: reckless planning; homogenized commerce that diminishes local flavor; scenes and settings forever lost and stubbornly remembered.

Yet out along those shady two-lane roads, it is yet possible to take in a setting not much different from that experienced by 19th Century travelers in their mule carts loaded down with King Cotton. Out there, native or newcomer will recognize unmistakably the spirited history and physical beauty that continues to define the essence of Tallahassee and set it apart.

South Florida has its sunsets, breezes and breathtaking layers of sophistication. But Tallahassee retains something old-fashioned and cherished: a certifiable edge of town. There city stops and countryside begins and everyone can briefly indulge in the illusion of what it was like when they were kids (wherever they were kids). There we can appreciate anew both that storied Southern charm and an ease with each other and with nature -- elements fiercely cherished here because sometimes both have been so hard-won.

Maybe it is merely that the kind of people who value these simple things -- family, nature, sense of community -- gravitate to Tallahassee while those whose ambitions call for something more drop in, look around and as quickly as they can move on.

But for the former, it takes only a little literary deceit to persuade ourselves that North Florida must have been what the essayist E.B. White had in mind when in the '40s he wrote, "I love Florida as much for the remains of her unfinished cities as for the bright cabanas on her beaches."

Unfinished cities such as ours, perchance? We're not everything that we hope to be one day, yet we're rich with the remains of what we've always been.

Those canopy roads, for example, are now protected by law. Beyond that, they are part of our lore: old Indian trails, which became market roads that plantation owners lined with live oaks. Now their branches meet above the roads in a dense overstory of growth dripping ghostly Spanish moss. Light beams filter down through them by day, supplying sunny fuel for dogwoods, azaleas, wild rhododendrons and magnolias, and they become spellbinding tunnels of darkness on moonless nights.

St. Augustine Road, southeast from downtown Tallahassee, dates back to the 1600s when it linked Spanish missions here to St. Augustine. No trace of a 17th Century Franciscan mission or Indian council house remains along this road, but the scenic beauty endures.

Miccosukee Road, extending into east-northeast Tallahassee, once connected two large Indian settlements and by the 1850s was used by 30 Leon County plantation owners to haul cotton to market. About 3.5 miles past Goodwood, the beauty of the canopy is clearly evident.

Centerville Road is quickly reached from the heart of town where Magnolia Drive ends and the canopy almost immediately begins to shade and soothe urban travelers who can hardly help complain of gridlock, but more would complain if Centerville's fine canopy was ever destroyed. And one of its best features belongs to the patient traveler: stop at Bradley's Country Store, a living landmark.

Meridian Road's history began in 1824 when a federal surveyor laid lengths of chain north through a Tallahassee woods to establish the Prime Meridian for surveying all of Florida. As a result of that surveyor's intent to go straight over a hill rather than around it, Meridian rarely dips or curves and has banks sometimes eight feet high.

Old Bainbridge Road -- where archaeologists found remains of native American villages and a 1600's Spanish mission -- is more or less parallel to Highway 27. It provides a more scenic route to Havana, which has become an emerging arts and antique center that is another nearby reminder of times that Tallahassee hearts still treasure.

While the physical majesty of surrounding countryside heightens our sense of place and gives Tallahassee a strong sense of identity, its internal urban mix of old and new, of different cultures, influences and interests adds layers of character that assure community vitality. Almost unbelievably, as Tallahassee's size has expanded, so has its tolerance for diversity, for each other. It blends university communities with their cultural bonuses and star-studded athletic programs with the contemporary urgency of a government center, and the result is stimulating public debate on generally forward-thinking community issues.

That's the mix which beguiles newcomers who may arrive here to attend Florida State or Florida A&M Universities or burgeoning Tallahassee Community College; who may be transferred here by private employers, or recruited by state government with each change of political command.

They come here for awhile and almost inevitably begin to feel that they're utterly welcome and could have been here forever. Soon they start making plans to stay here exactly that long.

Of course some who arrived reluctantly joke years later that Tallahassee is the Tar Baby of the South: *the harder you fight it, the harder you stick*. But countless others -- and I consider them among the membership of my mythical I-Came-Back-Club -- never fought too hard at all. On the contrary, so many of us have lived here awhile, moved away for personal or professional opportunities -- and then found ourselves spending months and years trying to figure out a way to come back.

And why not? The part of Florida with the Southern accent couples pastoral pleasures with the largesse of big cities -- though, as it has been gently noted, "everything is here, but to scale."

The wild beauty of wetlands, piney woods, cypress swamps and palm hammocks leads right straight to the Gulf of Mexico, famous Wakulla Springs -- one of the world's largest and deepest -- and St. Mark's National Wildlife Refuge, with its 65,000 acres of protected nature.

In the 28 miles between Tallahassee and Thomasville, Georgia, there exists not only the inimitable Maclay Gardens State Park with its profusion of midwinter blooms, but also America's largest number of original plantations -- 71 at last count. No Disney World mogul could recreate such rich authenticity.

But what visitors and newcomers love most, and what natives take huge pride in, is that the city has an almost palpable small-town friendliness. Although it is growing at a pace rivaling the condo-lined beaches and high-rise centers of South Florida, Tallahassee seems intent on nuturing growth that is of a human scale -- many more stories down to earth.

Indeed, the community is a place where nurseries and garden centers are big business. Residents here cherish home and family life, hours spent in their back yards and front yards, and also enjoying a park system that's the envy of many communities twice our size. In countless areas of the city, an utterly old-fashioned sense of neighborhood prevails, providing reassurance, security and new-fashioned Southern hospitality.

In the spirit of such geniality, <u>Under the Canopy</u> now falls into your hands.

Mary Ann Lindley

Appetizers
&
Beverages

Old Capitol

In 1823, the Legislature for the new Territory of Florida desired a permanent and central meeting place. William Pope DuVal, the first civilian governor of the Territory of Florida, sent one explorer on horseback from St. Augustine and another by boat from Pensacola to rendezvous. They met near a waterfall at a place the Creek and Seminole Indians called "Tallahassee." The meeting place was declared Florida's capital.

The Old Capitol was built in 1845 and expanded periodically. The dome, porticoes, north and south wings, steam heat, and red-and-white candy striped awnings were added in 1902. Although the Old Capitol was threatened with demolition during the 1970's, Floridians resolved to preserve the landmark. In 1978, the Legislature voted to restore the building to its 1902 splendor.

CLAM DIP

1   (8 ounce) package cream cheese
½   cup sour cream
2   teaspoons horseradish
    dash tabasco
    good sprinkle of salt
    good sprinkle of garlic powder
1   can minced clams

Blend first six ingredients together with small amount of clam juice (not too runny). Drain clams well and add to mixture. Beat with mixer. Chill and serve with chips or pretzels.

Vilma Wollschlager

CRAB DIP

1   (8 ounce) package cream cheese
1   jar cocktail sauce
1   teaspoon Worcestershire sauce
1   can crab meat, drained

Soften cream cheese and add Worcestershire sauce. Spread into shallow bowl or small tray. Layer with cocktail sauce. Mix crab with more cocktail sauce and spread on top.

Mary Brown

HOT CRAB MEAT SHERRY DIP

    3   (8 ounce) packages cream cheese, softened
    ¼   cup onion, minced
    ½   teaspoon parsley
    1   tablespoon sherry
    1   cup slivered almonds
        salt and pepper to taste
    1   pound fresh crab meat (carefully check for shells)

Heat cream cheese over low heat until melted, stir frequently. Add all ingredients except crab meat and blend. Add crab meat and blend well. Pour into a chafing dish or bowl that can be kept warm. Serve with crackers or cocktail rye bread.

Julie Blankenship

CRAB MEAT CON QUESO DIP

    ¾   cup chopped onion
    ¾   cup chopped green pepper
    1   garlic clove, minced
    1   tablespoon vegetable oil
    ½   cup picante sauce
    ½   pound pasteurized process cheese spread (regular or
        Mexican)
    ¼   pound crab meat (carefully check for shells)
    ½   cup chopped tomato

Sauté onion, green pepper and garlic in oil. Stir in picante sauce and heat thoroughly. Add cheese, cut into chunks. Cook until cheese melts. Gradually stir in crab meat and tomato. Heat and serve with plain tortillas or crackers. Also good over vegetables.

Debi Barrett-Hayes

JOAN'S AWARD WINNING SHRIMP DIP

½ cup mayonnaise
¼ teaspoon salt
1 can tiny shrimp (drained)
1 heaping teaspoon horseradish
3 teaspoons chili sauce
½ cup sour cream
½ cup grated onion
½ teaspoon paprika
1 can artichoke hearts, drained and chopped
  dash Worcestershire sauce
  dash Tabasco

Mix all ingredients. Refrigerate at least 2 hours. Garnish with sliced green olives. Serve with shredded wheat crackers.

Diane Winzler

TAHINI (SESAME PASTE DIP)

2 cloves garlic, crushed
  salt to taste
  juice of 2 lemons
½ cup tahini (sesame seed paste)
  pinch of ground cumin
1 tablespoon parsley, finely chopped

Crush garlic and salt together. Mix with a little lemon juice and blend in a blender or food processor with the sesame seed paste. Add cumin and remaining lemon juice to form a smooth paste. Serve in a bowl and garnish with parsley. Delicious with flatbread.

Julie Blankenship

BLACK BEAN DIP

 1 can black bean soup
 1 (8 ounce) package cream cheese
 1 small onion, chopped (can substitute green onions)
 2 teaspoons mayonnaise
 2 teaspoons parsley
    dash of Worcestershire sauce

Mix all ingredients together with an electric mixer. Add more cream cheese, if desired. Mixture will thicken after refrigeration. Serve with nacho/tortilla chips and picante sauce.

Diane Mann

HEATED MEXICAN DIP

 1 pound package pork sausage, hot
 1 small onion, chopped
 1 can cream of mushroom soup
 1 (8 ounce) jar picante sauce
 1 (1 pound) Mexican pasteurized process cheese spread

Cook meat and onion. In a crock pot, mix meat, onion, mushroom soup, picante sauce and cheese. Serve with tortilla chips or toasted pita triangles.

Variation: Ground beef can be used instead of pork.

Julie Rackley

CHALUPA (LAYERED DIP)

        1   (16 ounce) can refried beans
        ½   cup taco sauce
        2   small avocados
        2   teaspoons lime juice
        ¼   teaspoon garlic salt
        1   (2 ½ ounce) can chopped black olives
     1 ½   cups chopped green onions
        1   cup sour cream
     1 ½   cups tomato, finely chopped
        2   cups cheddar cheese, grated

Combine beans and taco sauce until mixture stirs easily. Spread evenly in 9x12 inch casserole dish. Peel and mash avocados. Add lime juice and garlic salt. Spread over bean mixture. Layer olives, green onions, sour cream, tomatoes and cheddar cheese. Serve with tortilla chips.

Wendy S. Matthews   *20 servings*

AUNT JOYCE'S DIP

        1   (8 ounce) package cream cheese, softened
        1   tablespoon mayonnaise
        1   tablespoon frozen chives
        ¼   cup nuts, finely chopped

Mix ingredients and refrigerate overnight. Serve with crackers or vegetables.

Variation: Season with ¼ teaspoon of garlic powder.

Janyce Horton   *6 servings*

CHEESE DIP

    ¾   pound hamburger
    1   pound box of pasteurized process cheese spread
    1   small can evaporated milk
  2-3   tablespoons salsa jalapeno relish
    2   tablespoons margarine

Brown hamburger and drain. Melt cheese. Add milk, salsa and margarine. Add hamburger. Serve warm with tortilla chips.

Sally Baker

CHEESY GARLIC ARTICHOKE DIP

    1   can artichokes, non-marinated
    2   tablespoons light margarine
    1   tablespoon garlic, pre-crushed in jar
  2-4   ounces sharp cheddar cheese, shredded
    ½   cup Parmesan cheese
    1   teaspoon lemon juice

In a food processor or blender, combine the artichokes, garlic, lemon juice, half of the cheddar cheese and ¼ cup Parmesan cheese. Grind until chopped medium fine. Transfer to oven or microwave safe bowl. Sprinkle remainder of the cheeses on top. Heat in a 350° oven for 10 minutes, or microwave on HIGH for 2-3 minutes until cheese is melted.

Kathleen Brennan

VIDALIA ONION DIP

        5   jumbo Vidalia onions
        1   cup sugar
      ½   cup white vinegar
        2   cups water
      ½   cup mayonnaise
      ½   teaspoon celery salt
      ½   teaspoon celery seed

Slice onions into thin rings, then cut rings in half. Mix together sugar, vinegar and water. Mix in onions. Marinate in refrigerator for 24 hours. Drain well. Mix onions with mayonnaise, celery salt and celery seed. Serve on crackers.

Sally Baker

"SKINNY" DIP FOR VEGETABLES OR CRACKERS

        1   envelope ranch dressing mix
        8   ounces low fat or fat free mayonnaise/salad dressing
        8   ounces low fat or fat free sour cream
      16   ounces low fat small curd cottage cheese

Mix all ingredients together with a mixer or in a blender. Serve chilled with raw vegetables or crackers.

Kim Cooper

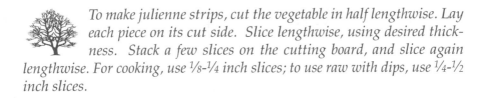

To make julienne strips, cut the vegetable in half lengthwise. Lay each piece on its cut side. Slice lengthwise, using desired thickness. Stack a few slices on the cutting board, and slice again lengthwise. For cooking, use ⅛-¼ inch slices; to use raw with dips, use ¼-½ inch slices.

VEGETABLE DIP

  1   cup mayonnaise
  ½ cup sour cream
  ¼ teaspoon salt
  1   teaspoon dried basil, oregano and thyme mixture, crushed
  ⅛ teaspoon curry powder
  1   tablespoon fresh minced parsley
  1   tablespoon onion, finely grated
  ½ teaspoon lemon juice
  ½ teaspoon Worcestershire sauce

Combine all ingredients. Chill at least 1 hour before serving. Serve with assorted raw vegetables (carrots, zucchini strips, celery).

Elaine K. Shapiro   *1 ½ cups*

SPINACH DIP

  1   (10 ounce) package frozen chopped spinach, thawed and
       squeezed dry
  1   package vegetable soup mix
  1   pint sour cream
  ½ cup mayonnaise
  ½ teaspoon lemon juice
  1   (8 ounce) can water chestnuts, finely chopped
  3   green onions, finely chopped

Mix soup mix, sour cream, mayonnaise and lemon juice. Stir in spinach, water chestnuts and onions. Cover and refrigerate 2 hours. Serve with corn chips.

Variation: Add ¼ teaspoon of white pepper.

CHIPPED BEEF DIP

8	ounces dried beef, chopped
2	(8 ounce) packages cream cheese
½	green pepper, chopped
2	tablespoons onion, minced
1	teaspoon Worcestershire sauce
¾	pint sour cream
¾	cup pecans, finely chopped
	garlic salt, to taste
	salt and pepper, to taste

Mix all ingredients except pecans. Put in a round 10-12 inch oven proof dish. Cover with pecans. Heat in a 350° oven for 30 minutes. Serve with shredded wheat crackers.

Tim Smawley

CHEESE BALL

1	clove garlic
¼	pound butter
1	(8 ounce) package cream cheese
1	(4 ounce) package sharp pasteurized process cheese spread
1 ½	ounces blue or Roquefort cheese
½	cup stuffed olives, chopped
	chopped pecans

Rub mixing bowl with garlic. Using hands, mix the butter, cream cheese and Old English cheese. Add the blue cheese and mix well. Add the olives. Chill and form into two balls. Cheese should be at room temperature when making the balls. Roll the balls in chopped pecans. May refrigerate for up to two weeks. Remove from refrigerator 1 hour before serving. Serve at room temperature.

Georgianna Wollschlager   *2 cheese balls*

EASY CHEESE WAFERS

½   pound sharp cheese, grated
¼   pound butter, creamed
1 ½ cups sifted flour
     pinch cayenne pepper
½   teaspoon salt

Mix together cheese, butter, salt and pepper. Add flour. Shape into a roll. Wrap in waxed paper and put in refrigerator. Will keep a month. When needed, slice into thin wafers and bake in a 350° oven. A pecan half, baked on each wafer, is decorative.

Marty Robinson

SEMINOLE CRACKERS

1   cup vegetable oil
1   package ranch dressing
½   teaspoon garlic salt
½   teaspoon lemon pepper
½   teaspoon dill weed
2   boxes oyster crackers

Mix oil, dressing mix and seasonings. Let stand for 30 minutes, stirring occasionally. Empty oyster crackers into brown bag (doubled). Pour oil over crackers, close bag and shake well. Pour into an air tight container. Let stand overnight.

Janyce Horton

PENUCHE NUTS

1	cup light brown sugar
½	cup white sugar
½	cup sour cream
1	teaspoon vanilla
2 ½	cups walnuts or pecans

Combine brown sugar, white sugar and sour cream. Stir well. Cook over medium heat until melted. Bring to a boil. Cook to soft ball stage. Add vanilla and nuts, stirring until mixture coats nuts. Pour on wax paper and separate nuts with a fork. Let cool. Store in air tight container.

Sally Baker

SPINACH BALLS

2	(10 ounce) packages frozen spinach
½	cup Parmesan cheese
3	cups packaged herb-seasoned stuffing mix
1	onion, finely chopped
¾	cup butter, melted
1 ½	teaspoon garlic salt
1	teaspoon pepper
6	eggs, well beaten

Cook spinach according to directions; drain. Add remaining ingredients and mix well. Shape into small balls. Bake in a 350° oven for 15-20 minutes. To freeze: place spinach balls on cookie sheet and put in freezer. When frozen, place in freezer-safe plastic bags and return to freezer.

Ann Boyd

CHUTNEY ROLL

  1 (8 ounce) package cream cheese, softened
 ½ cup chutney, finely chopped
 ½ cup chopped almonds, toasted
  1 tablespoon curry powder
 ½ teaspoon dry mustard
 ½ cup dry roasted peanuts, finely chopped

Combine first 5 ingredients in a mixing bowl; stir well. Shape into a log, wrap in foil and chill 1 hour. Mixture will be soft. Roll log in peanuts. Chill several hours or overnight. Serve with crackers.

Aileen Zaffaroni   *24 servings*

TIGER CATNIP

  2 (8 ounce) packages cream cheese
  1 (6 ounce) package wafer sliced roast beef
  3 large green onions, chopped
 ¾ teaspoon seasoned salt flavor enhancer
 ¾ teaspoon Worcestershire sauce
  1 cup chopped pecans

Mix all ingredients well, except pecans. Shape into a ball and roll in pecans.

Variation: Use light cream cheese for less calories.

Julia Moss Rhodes

CHILLED MEXICAN APPETIZER

1 (9 ounce) bean dip with jalapenos
1 (6 ounce) can tomato paste
1 (4 ounce) can chopped green chilies
1 ½ cups chopped tomatoes
1 cup sour cream
1 envelope taco mix
1 bunch green onions, chopped
1 large bell pepper, chopped
1 (2 ounce) jar diced pimiento
1 (2 ½ ounce) can chopped black olives
2 cups grated cheddar cheese

Combine bean dip, tomato paste and chilies. Spread evenly in 9x13 inch glass dish. Top evenly with chopped tomatoes. Combine sour cream and taco mix. Spread evenly over all. Combine onions, bell pepper, pimiento and olives. Sprinkle evenly over all. Top with grated cheese. Serve with tortilla or corn chips.

Kathy Wolff

HOLIDAY APPETIZER PIE

1 (8 ounce) package cream cheese, softened
1 (2 ½ ounce) jar sliced dried beef (rinse and dry off)
2 tablespoons green pepper, finely chopped
2 tablespoons onion, finely chopped
½ cup sour cream
½ cup walnuts, coarsely chopped

Blend cream cheese and sour cream. Chop dried beef and stir into cream cheese/sour cream mixture. Add onion and green pepper. Mix well and spoon into a 9 inch pie plate. Sprinkle walnuts over top. Bake for 15 minutes in a 350° oven. Cool and serve with assorted crackers.

Lucy Larson

CAVIAR APPETIZERS

> black caviar
> sour cream
> new potatoes, small

Boil potatoes in their skins until tender. Cool. Scoop out small hole on top and fill with sour cream. Sprinkle with caviar. Keep cool.

Brunetta Pfaender

SPICY MEATBALLS

MEATBALLS
> 2 pounds lean ground beef
> 2 eggs
> ½ cup bread crumbs or stuffing
> ½ cup water
> salt, pepper and garlic powder to taste

SAUCE
> juice of one lemon
> ½ cup grape jelly
> 12 ounces chili sauce

Mix all meatball ingredients together. Heat jelly and chili sauce until melted. Add lemon juice. Make small round meatballs from mixture and place in sauce. Cook on low heat for 45 minutes.

Cindy Mackiernan   *24 to 36 meatballs*

DEVILED HAM 'N EGG SALAD

    3   hard cooked eggs, chopped
    1   (4 ½ ounce) can deviled ham
    3   tablespoons mayonnaise
    3   tablespoons chopped onion
    2   tablespoons pickle relish
    8   slices white bread
    4   lettuce leaves
        black pepper

In a bowl, mix together chopped egg, ham, mayonnaise, onion and relish. Spread mixture on bread. Top each with a lettuce leaf and a slice of bread. Cut into quarters. Sprinkle sandwiches with black pepper.

Deborah Mayer   *4 servings*

LUAU BITES

    1   pound of bacon, cut into 1 ½ inch slices
    ¾   cup water chestnuts
    ¾   cup pineapple chunks
    ½   cup soy sauce
    4   tablespoons brown sugar

Wrap 1 ½ inch slices of bacon around water chestnuts or pineapple chunks. Fasten with toothpicks. Marinate in mixture of soy sauce and brown sugar for ½ hour. Broil, turning once, until bacon is crisp.

Julie Blankenship

CHICKEN PUFFS

1 package canned biscuits (5 count, flaky buttermilk style)
1 (5 ounce) can chunk chicken
½ cup cheddar cheese, shredded
⅓ cup walnuts
2 tablespoons chopped onion

Divide each biscuit into two parts to form 10 pieces. Place half these pieces as "bottoms" into greased muffin cups. Mix all ingredients and place a heaping tablespoon of mixture in cups. Top with the "tops" and press to seal edges. Bake in a 375° oven for 20 minutes or until golden brown.

Roberta Courtney

TERIYAKI CHICKEN WINGS

2 pounds chicken wings
1 (12 ounce) bottle teriyaki marinade
¼ cup water
4 cloves garlic, minced
¼ cup honey
1 large ziplock bag

Cut chicken wings into three pieces. Discard the tips. Place chicken pieces and all other ingredients into large ziplock bag. Mix well. Let marinade from 2-12 hours. Place wings in a shallow baking pan. Pour marinade over the wings. Bake in a 350° oven for 1 hour, or until brown. Turn wings after 30 minutes.

5 servings

HERBED CHICKEN WINGS

WINGS

- 2 pounds small chicken wings
- ⅓ cup lemon juice
- 1 clove minced garlic
- 1 teaspoon tarragon
- ½ teaspoon salt
- ¼ teaspoon black pepper
- ½ cup all-purpose flour
  vegetable oil for frying

DIP

- ½ cup mayonnaise
- ¾ cup fresh parsley leaves
- 2 tablespoons chopped green onion
- ½ cup sour cream
- 2 ounces blue cheese, crumbled
  pinch of ground red pepper

Cut wings into 3 pieces through joints. Discard wing tips, or wrap and freeze for chicken stock. In a large bowl, combine wings with lemon juice, garlic, tarragon, salt and pepper. Cover and marinate in refrigerator for at least 2 hours overnight. In a plastic bag, shake wings in flour. Preheat oil to 325°. Add wings and fry until brown and crisp, about 10 minutes. Drain, cool and refrigerate. Serve with dip. To prepare dip, combine mayonnaise, parsley leaves and onion in a blender or food processor. Blend until smooth. Fold in sour cream, blue cheese and red pepper. Transfer to storage container; cover and refrigerate.

4 to 6 servings

PICKUPS

½ pound soft margarine
3 tablespoons poppy seeds
1 medium onion, grated
3 tablespoons dry mustard
2 cans refrigerated crescent rolls
1 tablespoon Worcestershire sauce
1 pound corned beef, sliced thin
½ pound Swiss cheese, sliced into 24 pieces

Mix margarine, poppy seeds, onion, dry mustard and Worcestershire sauce. Unroll Crescent rolls and brush on mixture. Add a slice of corned beef and Swiss cheese and roll up. Brush the remaining mixture on top of each rollup Crescent. Bake for 10-15 minutes in a 350° oven.

24 servings

TRI STUFFED CELERY

½ cup shredded Swiss cheese
½ cup shredded cheddar cheese
2 tablespoons crumbled blue cheese
2 tablespoons mayonnaise
1 teaspoon Worcestershire sauce
 paprika
 celery sticks cut into 3 inch lengths

Blend first 5 ingredients in an electric blender or food processor. Stuff celery. Sprinkle with paprika. Refrigerate until ready to use.

Mary D. Beasley

SPINACH PATE

3 (10 ounce) packages frozen chopped spinach, thawed
¼ cup margarine
1 cup green onions, sliced
2 large carrots, shredded
1 cup half and half
1 teaspoon salt
1 teaspoon basil
¼ teaspoon cayenne pepper
4 eggs

Drain spinach, squeeze or press to remove water. Chop finely. Grease a loaf pan; line the bottom with foil. Melt margarine in a saucepan, then sauté onions and carrots until tender. Stir in spinach gradually. Add half and half, salt, basil and pepper. Bring to a boil. Remove from heat and stir in eggs. Spoon mixture into pan and cover with foil. Place loaf pan in a layer pan with water coming up to 1 inch on the outer side of the loaf pan to create a double boiler effect in your oven. Bake in a 375° oven for 1 hour and 15 minutes, or until knife inserted comes out clean. Cool and place something heavy (such as cans) on top of loaf and refrigerate overnight. Remove 15 minutes before serving. With a metal spatula, loosen pate. Remove foil from the bottom and slice. May be served with crackers or Toast Points.

TOAST POINTS

butter or margarine
bread, sliced thin

Trim crusts. Roll bread flat. Lightly butter and cut diagonally into quarters. Bake at 250° until crisp and lightly browned. Store for up to three days in airtight container. Use a variety of breads or cut bread into different shapes for more appeal.

VIRGINIA SETTLER'S PUNCH

    6   lemons, whole
    1   lemon, sliced thinly
    1   pint rum
    1   pint bourbon
1 ½   pounds sugar (add more to taste)
  3-6 cups strong green tea, chilled

Squeeze juice from lemons over sugar. Add cold tea. Add lemon rinds, with seeds removed, to the mixture. Let stand for several hours. Strain through cheesecloth. Add spirits. Garnish with thinly sliced lemon. Bottle and put on ice to chill.

PARTY PUNCH

    2   small packages lemon gelatin mix
    1   small can frozen lemonade concentrate
    1   large can frozen orange juice concentrate
   ¾   cup sugar
    2   large cans pineapple juice
    3   large bottles ginger ale
   ½   small bottle almond extract

Mix gelatin, lemonade and orange juice according to directions on packages. Mix in punch bowl. Add sugar. Mix well. Add pineapple juice, almond extract and ginger ale. Chill with cubes of any flavor frozen juice.

Ann Boyd   *75 servings*

AUNT HELEN MOORE'S CHAMPAGNE PUNCH

　2　cups sugar
　4　cups water
　½　cup lemon juice
　½　cup lime juice
4 ¼　cups orange juice
　2　cups grapefruit juice
　2　cups rhine wine
　1　quart champagne

Combine sugar with 2 cups of water and lemon juice. Boil 1 minute. Add remaining water. Cool. Stir in remaining juices. Chill. Pour into punch bowl over ice. Add wine and champagne just before serving. Garnish with thin lemon slices and mint leaves. (Garnish with limes and strawberries too, if desired).

1 gallon

MINT PUNCH

1　jar mint jelly
2　(46 ounce) cans pineapple juice
1　(2 liter) bottle ginger ale

Melt mint jelly in a pan over low heat. Add the melted jelly to the pineapple juice. Mix well. Refrigerate. When ready to serve, place the mint/pineapple mix into the punch bowl. At the very last moment add the ginger ale. You can freeze a small amount of the mix in a mold and add to the punch to keep it cool.

Clifton Quinly

ORANGE SPARKLER

  1 (12 ounce) can orange juice concentrate
3 ¾ cups water
  2 tablespoons lime juice
32 ounces lemon-lime soda
     orange slices

Combine orange juice concentrate, water and lime juice; stir well. Add lemon-lime soda just before serving. Serve over ice ring and garnish with orange slices.

Dianne Brantly

CRANBERRY PUNCH

  2 (6 ounce) cans frozen orange juice concentrate
  1 (6 ounce) can frozen lemonade concentrate
  1 quart pineapple juice
  4 pints cranberry juice
  3 cups sugar
11 cups water
  4 bottles ginger ale

Combine orange juice, lemonade, pineapple juice and cranberry juice. Combine sugar and 3 cups water in a pan and heat to make a syrup; cool. Add to juices. Just before serving add 8 cups of water and ginger ale.

Mildred Gardner

FRUIT PUNCH

- 1 bottle white wine
- 1 bottle champagne or cold duck
- 1 bottle ginger ale
   sugar to taste
   maraschino cherries
   fresh fruit of the season or 1 can of fruit

Cut fruit into bite-size pieces and sprinkle with sugar. Add wine, champagne, or cold duck and ginger ale. Serve very cold.

Trina McCarthy

MISTLETOE MULL

- 1 bottle hearty Burgundy
- 2 cups water
- 1 cup granulated sugar
- 4 sticks cinnamon
- 4 whole cloves
- 2 lemons or 1 lemon and 1 orange, thinly sliced

Boil water, sugar, cinnamon and cloves for 5 minutes. Add lemon slices. Let stand for 5 minutes. Add wine and heat slowly. Do not boil. Serve warm.

Betty Ashler

MULLED CIDER

       2 sticks cinnamon
      12 whole cloves
       2 teaspoons whole allspice
       1 gallon apple cider
       1 cup brown sugar, firmly packed
       1 lemon, thinly sliced

Tie the cinnamon sticks, cloves and allspice in a small cheesecloth bag. Place cider in a large, heavy enameled kettle; drop in the bag of spices and add brown sugar. Simmer, uncovered, for 15 minutes. Remove the bag of spices. Pour cider into a heatproof punch bowl; float lemon slices on top and serve hot.

Averell R. Tate

WASSAIL

       2 quarts sweet apple cider
       2 #2 cans pineapple juice
       1 teaspoon whole cloves
       1 cup lemon juice
       2 cups orange juice
       1 stick whole cinnamon
          sugar or honey to taste

Combine all ingredients. Bring to a simmer. Strain and serve hot.

Beverly Cliett   *20 to 25 servings*

ROSEMARY LEMONADE

2 heaping teaspoons fresh rosemary
½ cup honey
⅔ cup lemon juice
4 cups water

Simmer rosemary for 5 minutes in 1 cup water and ½ cup honey. Strain rosemary out of liquid. Add 3 cups cold water and lemon juice. Chill. Serve with lemon slices as garnish.

Margaret Rodrigue

COFFEE FRAPPE

4 ounces instant coffee
1 quart boiling water
1 ½ cups sugar
3 ½ quarts cold water
1 ½ quarts milk
1 ½ pints cream
⅛ teaspoon salt
1 gallon vanilla ice cream

Dissolve coffee in 1 quart boiling water; add sugar. Add 3 ½ quarts of cold water. Mix well. Add milk, cream and salt. Serve ½ of the coffee mixture with ½ of the ice cream. Leave remainder of the ice cream firm until ready to use with remaining coffee mixture.

Betty Lee

HOT CRANBERRY TEA

1 (32 ounce) bottle cranberry juice cocktail
1 package Red Hots candy
1 small can lemonade concentrate
1 small can orange juice concentrate
2 cups sugar
3 quarts water

Boil 2 quarts water, sugar and Red Hots until sugar and Red Hots are dissolved. Add cranberry juice cocktail, orange and lemonade concentrate, and 1 quart water. Serve hot.

Barbara Woolard   *1 gallon*

QUICK RUSSIAN TEA

1 (18 ounce) jar Tang
½ teaspoon instant tea mix
¾ cup sugar
½ teaspoon ground cloves
½ teaspoon ground cinnamon
½ teaspoon ground ginger

Mix above ingredients thoroughly. When ready to serve, place 2 heaping teaspoons of mixture into 1 cup hot water.

Hint: Store in an air tight container.

Wilda Charlette

Joy Morris

Soups
&
Salads

First Presbyterian Church

The First Presbyterian Church is Tallahassee's oldest house of worship and Florida's oldest public building in continuous years of service. The original building, which was dedicated on May 13, 1838, was financed by the sale of pews to members. "Old First," as it is commonly known, has been active in pivotal historical events. The church was regularly used as a town hall for political speeches and public orations during Florida's territorial period. In the 1840s, the church was used as a place of refuge for women and children when the men went out to guard against Indian uprisings. Four rifle slots are still visible in the basement's brick walls. During the Civil War, the congregation offered the Confederacy the steeple bell to melt down to make cannon balls, but the offer was declined. Nevertheless, the church welcomed slaves as independent members, with or without their masters' consent.

COLD PEACH SOUP WITH BLUEBERRIES

1 ½ cups water
  4 cloves, whole
  ¾ cup sugar
  1 cinnamon stick, broken into large pieces
  2 tablespoons cornstarch mixed with ¼ cup cold water
1 ½ cups dry white wine
  3 pounds ripe peaches, peeled and sliced
  1 cup fresh blueberries
  1 cup heavy cream, whipped

Pour water into 2 quart stockpot and add cloves, sugar and cinnamon. Bring to a boil. Reduce heat and simmer for 10 minutes. Add diluted cornstarch, whipping it into the syrup with a wire whisk. Bring to a boil again. Remove from stove, stir in wine and refrigerate until cool. Remove cloves and cinnamon from syrup. Add about 2 cups of the peaches to the syrup. Puree remaining peaches in a blender. Add pureed peaches to the syrup mixture and pour into a 5 quart container. Chill thoroughly. Garnish with blueberries and whipped cream.

Karen Macpherson   *6 to 8 servings*

 To puree, use a food processor, blender or food mill to grind food to a thick liquid or paste.

MOTHER'S CUCUMBER SOUP

1 ½   medium cucumbers, peeled, seeded and chopped into small cubes
  2   tablespoons of corn oil
  1   tablespoon chopped onion
  1   package chicken noodle soup mix
  3   cups of water
  2   teaspoons dill seed
 ½   pint sour cream
     dash of cayenne pepper
 ½   cucumber, sliced thin

Combine cucumber and onion in a small skillet and sauté in oil until tender. Prepare soup mix in water and boil until the noodles are soft. Add dill seed and cayenne pepper. Place cucumbers, onions and soup into blender and mix on low speed until smooth. Add sour cream and blend slowly again. Serve cold. Garnish with remaining cucumber and cayenne pepper.

Mildred Gabrielson   *4 servings*

Place spices to be removed before serving (such as bay leaves, whole cloves, garlic buds) into a metal teaball. The spices can then easily be removed as needed or before serving.

CHILI #1: HOT AND SPICY

- 2 pounds coarse ground round
- 1 large onion, chopped
- 1 green pepper, chopped
- 1 (8 ounce) can tomato sauce
- 1 cup water
- 1 tablespoon chili powder
- ¼ teaspoon cayenne pepper
- ½ teaspoon black pepper
- 1 teaspoon ground cumin
- ½ teaspoon oregano
- 2 cloves garlic, finely chopped
- 1 teaspoon salt
- 1 (16 ounce) can kidney beans, drained and rinsed
- 1 additional (16 ounce) can of kidney beans (optional)

Brown meat, onions and green pepper. Add remaining ingredients except kidney beans. Put on low heat in a 5 quart pot, simmering about 30 minutes. Add kidney beans. Can be served "as is" or over rice.

Mary J. Marchant   *8 servings*

 For hot dog lovers, fill disposable bathroom cups ¾ full with left-over chili, cover and freeze. When thawed and reheated, each cup is enough to cover one hot dog generously.

CHILI #2: MEATLESS CHILI

       2   tablespoons corn oil
   1 ¼   cups onion, chopped
       2   cloves garlic, minced
       2   tablespoons chili powder
       ¼   teaspoon dried basil leaves
       ¼   teaspoon dried oregano leaves
       ¼   teaspoon ground cumin
       2   cups diced zucchini
       1   cup diced carrots
       2   pounds tomatoes, cut in eighths
       1   (20 ounce) can chickpeas, drained
       1   (16 ounce) can kidney beans, undrained

In a 5 quart stockpot, heat corn oil over medium heat. Add next 6 ingredients. Cook, stirring, 5 minutes or until onion is tender. Add zucchini and carrots. Cook, stirring for 2 minutes. Stir in remaining ingredients. Bring to a boil. Reduce heat and simmer 30-35 minutes.

Nancy Hoppe   *6 servings*

When chopping onions, chill thoroughly first (either in the refrigerator or 10-15 minutes in the freezer). A cold onion releases fewer eye irritants.

PICCADILLO (SPANISH STEW)

1 pound Italian sausage
1 pound ground chuck
1 pound chicken breasts, boned and skinless
½ cup olive oil
4 onions, sliced
3 cloves garlic
1 (24 ounce) can tomatoes
1 (12 ounce) can tomato paste
2 green peppers, diced
1 (6 ounce) can green chilies, drained
1 (10 ounce) jar whole olives, drained
¾ cup raisins
1 teaspoon Worcestershire sauce
4 tablespoons salsa
1 bay leaf
season to taste with: salt, pepper, basil, oregano

Slice sausage and cut chicken into bite size pieces. Brown meat in olive oil. In a 5 quart stockpot, add meat and remaining ingredients. Simmer for 30 minutes.

Serving Suggestion: Serve over yellow rice accompanied with a green salad and crusty bread to make a hearty meal.

Kay Luger   *10 to 12 servings*

CHICKEN AND PASTA STEW

4 medium chicken breasts, chopped into bite size pieces
1 cup corkscrew pasta
1 cup spinach corkscrew pasta
1 (15 ounce) can stewed tomatoes
1 (15 ounce) can chicken broth
1 small onion, chopped
1 (20 ounce) package chopped frozen vegetables
1 (16 ounce) can kidney beans, drained
1 teaspoon pepper
½ teaspoon salt
1 teaspoon garlic powder
1 teaspoon hot sauce

In a 5 quart stockpot, combine all ingredients. Bring to a boil for 3 minutes, stirring often. Simmer, covered, for 30-35 minutes.

Susan Swartz   *8 servings*

BRIE SOUP

4 large onions, thinly sliced
3 tablespoons butter, melted
¼ teaspoon salt
4 cups beef broth
⅓ cup dry Madeira
4 ounces Brie cheese

In 4 quart sauce pot, sauté onions in butter. Add salt and cover tightly. Cook over low heat until tender; do not brown onions. Add broth and simmer for 20 minutes. Add Madeira. Dice cheese and place in bottom of soup cups and cover with hot soup.

Karen Macpherson   *6 servings*

HOT AND SOUR SOUP

  4   cups chicken stock
  6   ounces chicken, cut into julienne strips
  ½   cup tofu, cut into julienne strips
  ½   cup bamboo shoots, cut into julienne strips
6-8   whole mushrooms, thinly sliced
  1   tablespoon light soy sauce
  ¼   teaspoon sugar
  2   tablespoons cornstarch, mixed with 3 tablespoons water
  1   egg, beaten slightly
  3   tablespoons Chinese red vinegar or rice vinegar
  ½   teaspoon ground white pepper
  2   green onions, thinly sliced

Bring stock to a boil in an uncovered 5 quart stockpot. Add chicken, tofu, bamboo shoots, mushrooms. Cook 3-5 minutes. Mix soy sauce, sugar and cornstarch. Add mixture to soup, stir and bring to a light boil. Slowly stir in egg. Turn off heat. Put vinegar and pepper in bowl. Add soup and green onions. Stir and serve immediately. For a zestier taste, add hot red pepper in bowl.

Judy Wheaton   *6 servings*

Canned consommé, chicken broth, beef broth and clam juice can be used in place of basic stocks or consommés. Commercially prepared stocks are usually saltier than homemade stocks. Use wine, beer or tomato juice to dilute.

POTATO SOUP WITH RIVELS

  1 quart chicken broth
  4 medium potatoes, unpeeled and diced
  1 tablespoon butter
  1 quart milk
  ¼ cup celery leaves, chopped
     salt and freshly ground black pepper to taste
  1 egg, beaten
  1 cup flour

Bring the chicken stock to a boil in a 4 quart stockpot. Add the diced potatoes and cook until tender. Add the butter, milk and celery leaves and simmer. Add salt and pepper. In a small bowl, stir the beaten egg into the flour with a fork until it becomes a grainy mixture. Sprinkle small amounts at a time into soup, stirring constantly with a wooden spoon. Cook the rivels in soup for 15 minutes. Be careful, as the rivels may lump up.

Candy Mitchell   *8 servings*

You will need less salt in soups if it is added at the end of cooking. This will season the broth rather than the other ingredients and give the taste sensation of more salt.

BROCCOLI SOUP

  1   pound fresh broccoli, trimmed
  1   small onion, chopped
4-5   sprigs parsley, chopped
  1   teaspoon salt
  1   tablespoon chives, chopped
  ¼   teaspoon cayenne pepper
  2   stalks celery with leaves, chopped
  1   large carrot, diced
  1   quart chicken broth
  2   tablespoons cornstarch

Cook broccoli with next 8 ingredients in a 4 quart stockpot. Bring to a boil, then simmer 20 minutes or until broccoli is tender. Mix cornstarch with a little bit of water in a small cup. Stir until smooth, then add to pot. Simmer for 30-40 minutes. May be frozen for later use.

Adeline Barrack   *6 servings*

Many soups freeze well. Freeze it in individual portions in boilable plastic freezer bags. Then, for a quick-to-fix soup, toss the bag into boiling water. Or defrost it and serve cold.

PUMPKIN SOUP

1 cup chopped onion
¼ cup margarine
1 (29 ounce) can pumpkin
1 (16 ounce) can pumpkin
6 cups canned chicken broth
1 (12 ounce) can evaporated milk
¼ teaspoon salt
¼ teaspoon dried marjoram
¼ teaspoon dried thyme
6 dashes hot pepper sauce

In a 5 quart stockpot, cook onion in margarine until tender. Add pumpkin. Gradually stir in chicken broth. Add evaporated milk, spices and hot sauce. Bring to a boil, then reduce heat. Simmer uncovered for 5 minutes, stirring occasionally.

Serving Suggestions:
Top each serving with either toasted pumpkin seeds, sprigs of fresh herbs, or a tablespoon of yogurt.

Beth Hamilton   *10 to 12 servings*

Creativity is part of the fun in entertaining. The pumpkin soup, above, can be served cold in a hollowed and cleaned pumpkin shell. A seafood soup can be served from a clean, small fish bowl. Cream soups can even be served from a pitcher.

BLACK BEAN SOUP

1 pound dried black beans
3 quarts water
1 slice of white bacon or hamhock
3 tablespoons olive oil
2 onions, chopped
1 large green pepper, chopped
3 teaspoons sugar
2 teaspoons cider vinegar
2 tablespoons salt

Pick and wash black beans. Add water to beans in a 5 quart stockpot and cook until almost tender. Add more water if needed. Sauté bacon, salt, garlic, onions and pepper in olive oil. Add salt and one teaspoon sugar. Pour this mixture into black beans when they are almost tender, then add 2 more teaspoons of sugar and 2 teaspoons of vinegar. Cook for 30 minutes. May be served over white rice and garnished with chopped raw onion. May also be served with crackers or cornbread.

Mrs. Joseph A. Boyd, Jr.   *6 servings*

To prepare rice ahead of time, boil for ¾ the normal cooking time. Drain excess liquid and store, covered, in the refrigerator. To finish cooking, steam white rice for 5-7 minutes, brown rice for 10-12 minutes.

CURRIED SHRIMP AND RICE SALAD

   1   package chicken flavored rice vermicelli mix
  ½   pound cooked and peeled shrimp
   1   (6 ounce) jar marinated artichoke hearts, quartered
   1   large green pepper, chopped
   4   green onions, chopped
  12   stuffed olives, whole
  ⅓   cup mayonnaise
  ¼   teaspoon curry powder
   1   teaspoon olive juice
   1   teaspoon Worcestershire sauce
   1   teaspoon wine vinegar

Prepare rice vermicelli mix according to package directions. In a 2 quart bowl, add remaining ingredients. Mix thoroughly. Chill until ready to serve.

Serving Suggestion: Enhanced flavor is obtained by preparing this salad 24 hours before serving. Will keep for up to 3 days. Travels well for picnics and outdoor activities.

Ann Bruce   *4 servings*

EGGPLANT AUBERGINE

   1   eggplant, large enough to make 1 cup pulp
  ½   onion, finely chopped
   2   tablespoons mayonnaise or olive oil
       salt and pepper to taste
       juice of ½ lemon

Place eggplant on an open flame and let it burn on all sides until soft. Cool and peel. Mash pulp with fork until it is like a paste. Add onion, salt, pepper and lemon juice. Stir in mayonnaise or olive oil or 1 tablespoon of each. Mix well. Serve on a lettuce leaf as an appetizer. Garnish with slices of tomato and cucumber.

Irma S. Horn   *6 to 8 servings*

APRICOT-PINEAPPLE SALAD

2 (3 ounce) packages apricot gelatin
1 cup mini marshmallows
2 cups boiling water
2 cups cold water
1 (20 ounce) can crushed pineapple
2 bananas, mashed

TOPPING

1 egg, beaten
1 tablespoon flour
½ cup sugar
2 tablespoons butter
1 (8 ounce) package cream cheese, softened
1 (9 ounce) package frozen whipped topping, thawed
½ cup chopped pecans

Dissolve marshmallows and gelatin in boiling water, add cold water. In a 9x13 inch pan, mix in drained pineapple (save juice) and bananas. Refrigerate until firm. For topping, combine egg, flour, sugar, pineapple juice and butter in a saucepan. Cook over medium heat until thick. Fold in cream cheese and mix well. Fold whipped topping into cream cheese mixture. Spread evenly on top of firm jello mixture. Sprinkle pecans on top. Chill until ready to serve.

10 to 12 servings

SHIMMERING WINTER SALAD

    1   (17 ounce) can fruit cocktail
    1   can mandarin oranges, drained
    1   (3 ounce) package lime gelatin
    1   cup sour cream

Drain juice from fruit cocktail and add water to make 1 cup. Heat in saucepan. Dissolve gelatin in hot liquid. Cool until mixture mounds on spoon. Fold in sour cream, fruit cocktail and mandarin oranges. Pour into a mold and chill until firm.

Shari Cromar   *4 to 6 servings*

CONGEALED CRANBERRY-SOUR CREAM SALAD

    2   (3 ounce) packages cherry gelatin
    1   cup hot water
    1   envelope Knox gelatin
    ¼   cup cold water
    1   (20 ounce) can crushed pineapple, drained with juice saved
    2   (16 ounce) cans jellied cranberry sauce
    1   (8 ounce) carton sour cream
    1   cup pecans, chopped

Dissolve cherry gelatin in 1 cup hot water, then add 1 cup of pineapple juice. Dissolve gelatin in ¼ cup cold water. Add gelatin to cherry pineapple mixture; blend well. Mash cranberry sauce with a fork until smooth. Place sour cream in a serving dish, add gelatin mixture slowly, stirring until smooth. Add cranberry sauce, crushed pineapple and chopped pecans. Mix thoroughly and chill until firm.

Nelle Sewell   *8 to 10 servings*

STRAWBERRY PECAN CONGEALED SALAD

- 2 (3 ounce) packages strawberry gelatin
- 1 cup boiling water
- 1 (20 ounce) can crushed pineapple
- 2 (10 ounce) packages frozen strawberries, thawed
- 1 cup pecans, chopped
- 1 pint sour cream

Dissolve gelatin in boiling water. Gently fold in the strawberries, pineapple with juice, and nuts. Pour ½ of mixture into an 8x12 inch pan and refrigerate until firm. Layer sour cream on top. Gently add other half of mixture. Refrigerate until firm.

Martha Eacker   *8 to 10 servings*

WESTERN CHICKEN SALAD

- ¾ cup mayonnaise
- 1 teaspoon ground ginger (optional)
- ½ teaspoon salt
- 3 cups cubed, cooked chicken
- 1 ½ cups red seedless grapes, halved
- 1 cup celery, chopped
- ½ cup sliced green onions
- ½ cup chopped walnuts

In a 3 quart bowl, combine mayonnaise, ginger and salt. Stir in remaining ingredients. May garnish with additional walnuts if desired.

Nancy Sutton   *4 servings*

BLUE CRAB SALAD

 ½ cup mayonnaise
 ½ teaspoon Cajun spice
 ½ teaspoon black pepper
 1 medium green pepper, chopped
 ½ cup sour cream
 ½ teaspoon tarragon
1 ½ pounds cooked crab meat, cut into bite-size pieces
 ½ teaspoon basil
 ¼ small onion, chopped
 2 stalks celery, chopped
 ¼ teaspoon salt
 ½ teaspoon garlic powder

In a 2 quart bowl, mix all ingredients together. Serve with celery and carrot sticks or with crackers.

4 to 6 servings

DILLED TUNA SALAD

 1 (12 ounce) can white albacore tuna, drained
 ¼ cup plain yogurt
 ¼ cup honey mustard
 ⅛ cup mayonnaise
 1 cup thinly sliced celery
 ¼ cup chopped green onion
 ⅓ cup sliced almonds
 2 teaspoons dill weed
 ¼ teaspoon white pepper
 4 ounces sliced water chestnuts

In a 2 quart serving bowl, mix all ingredients together thoroughly and serve.

Debi Barrett-Hayes   *4 servings*

3 BEAN SALAD

        1   can green beans, drained
        1   can yellow wax beans, drained
        1   can kidney beans, drained and washed
        2   bell peppers, chopped
        1   onion, chopped
        ½   cup vinegar
        ¾   cup sugar
        ½   teaspoon pepper
            dash hot pepper sauce
        1   teaspoon salt
        ½   cup oil

In a 2 quart bowl, mix beans with bell pepper and onion. Mix vinegar, sugar, pepper, hot pepper sauce, salt and oil together. Pour over bean mixture and mix well. Cover and refrigerate until ready to serve.

Jane Rowan   *6 servings*

CAULIFLOWER SALAD

        1   head cauliflower, cut into bite-size pieces
        1   medium onion, chopped
        ½   cup mayonnaise
        ½   cup bacon, crumbled
        ⅓   cup Parmesan cheese

In a 3 quart bowl, mix all ingredients together and serve. May be served on lettuce.

Connie Brown   *6 to 8 servings*

HERBED WHITE BEAN SALAD

   1   pound small dry white beans
   2   quarts water
   1   teaspoon salt
   1   tablespoon olive oil
   2   medium tomatoes, chopped and seeded
  ½   cup chopped red onion
  ⅔   cup pitted black olives, sliced
   6   tablespoons olive oil
   6   tablespoons white wine vinegar
   2   large cloves garlic, minced
   1   tablespoon dried basil, crumbled
       salt and pepper to taste

Rinse beans. Simmer beans in a 4 quart saucepan with water, salt and olive oil about 1 ½ hours. Drain and cool slightly. Combine beans with remaining ingredients, except basil. Mix well. Cover and refrigerate until well chilled. Mix in basil before serving.

Shirley Unger   *12 servings*

FRUIT BOWL

   2   bananas, peeled and sliced
   2   medium oranges, peeled and sectioned
   1   cup strawberries, halved

DRESSING
  ½   cup sour cream
   1   tablespoon honey
   1   tablespoon orange juice

Combine fruit in a 2 quart bowl, cover and refrigerate for 1 hour. Combine dressing ingredients and refrigerate 1 hour. Pour dressing over fruit and toss.

                                        4 servings

FRUIT SLAW

        1   small cabbage, sliced
        1   medium apple, chopped
        1   (11 ounce) can mandarin oranges
        ½   cup grapes, halved
        ¼   cup raisins
        ⅓   cup honey
        3   tablespoons lemon juice
        1   teaspoon celery or poppy seed
        ½   teaspoon dry mustard
        ½   teaspoon paprika
        ¼   teaspoon salt
        ½   cup salad oil

In a 3 quart bowl, stir together cabbage and fruits. Cover and chill. In blender, mix honey, lemon juice and spices. Gradually add oil and blend for 1 ½ minutes or until mixture is slightly thick. Cover dressing and chill. Add dressing to salad and toss gently. Serve immediately.

8 to 10 servings

To chop slaw in the blender, wash and quarter cabbage head, removing center stem. Cut each quarter into smaller pieces. Fill blender container half full of cabbage, then fill completely with water. With the top on the blender, turn on and off quickly until cabbage is chopped to desired size. Drain into colander. Repeat until all cabbage is chopped.

ICE BOX SLAW

    1   head cabbage, shredded
    1   green pepper, chopped
    2   medium onions, chopped
    1   cup sugar
    ¾   cup salad oil
    1   cup vinegar
1 ½   tablespoons salt
    2   teaspoons celery seed
    1   teaspoon dry mustard

Combine cabbage, green pepper and onion in a 3 quart bowl. In a separate saucepan, combine sugar, salad oil, vinegar, salt, celery seed and dry mustard. Bring to a boil. Pour sauce over cabbage mixture. Do not stir. Refrigerate 12 hours before serving.

8 to 10 servings

LAYERED SPINACH SALAD

    1   bunch fresh spinach, torn
    ½   head lettuce, torn
    1   bunch green onions, chopped
    1   (10 ounce) can English peas, drained
    1   pound fresh mushrooms, sliced
    ½   pound bacon, cooked and crumbled
    1   (8 ounce) bottle ranch style dressing

In a 3 quart bowl, layer ingredients in the following order: spinach, lettuce, green onions, English peas, mushrooms, bacon. Top with ranch dressing. Refrigerate at least 8 hours and serve.

Ada Dee Stephenson   *6 to 8 servings*

Breads

Old City Cemetery

The Florida Territorial Council established the Old City Cemetery in 1829. A system of squares and lots was devised in 1841 to maintain order and sanitation when a yellow fever epidemic swept through Tallahassee. In addition, the cemetery was segregated in 1841 with white burials restricted to the eastern section and burial of slaves and free people of color confined to the western section. Religious denominations were also assigned to certain areas.

Old City Cemetery is the burial place for a diverse 19th century population - governors, educators, merchants, Civil War soldiers, ordained ministers, prominent leaders, pioneers, and slaves. Although the grave markers serve as memorials to those who have died, they also serve as an artistic portrayal of attitudes concerning death and resurrection during the 19th century. Grave markers in Old City Cemetery include simple stone tablets, distinctive obelisks, box tombs, and ornate cast iron fences. The Old City Cemetery is listed on the National Register of Historic Places.

WAFFLES

        2   cups flour
        ½   teaspoon salt
        3   teaspoons baking powder
        2   eggs, separated
        ½   cup shortening
    1 ¾   cups milk

Sift dry ingredients together, add egg yolks and milk. Beat egg whites until stiff. Add shortening to flour, egg yolk and milk mixture. Fold in egg whites. Pour evenly into a greased waffle iron. Cook until brown.

Jo Bevis

REFRIGERATOR BRAN MUFFINS

        6   cups ready to eat bran cereal (your choice)
        2   cups boiling water
        1   cup margarine
    1 ½   cups sugar
        4   eggs
        1   quart buttermilk
        5   cups flour
        5   teaspoons baking soda
        1   teaspoon salt

Place 2 cups cereal in bowl and add boiling water, let cool. Cream together in a large mixing bowl margarine, sugar and eggs. Beat in buttermilk to soaked bran mixture. Sift together flour, baking soda and salt. Add dry ingredients to bran mixture and fold until flour is moistened. Fold in remaining 4 cups of bran cereal. Store batter in covered container in refrigerator. Will keep 3-4 weeks. When ready to bake, preheat oven to 400°, fill greased muffin tins ⅔ full and bake 20 minutes. May add raisins and/or nuts just before baking if desired.

Ruth Peck   *12 servings*

FRUITY MUFFINS

1 cup flour
½ cup quick oats
1 teaspoon baking powder
1 teaspoon cinnamon
¼ teaspoon salt
1 large egg
¾ cup brown sugar
¼ cup margarine, melted
1 teaspoon vanilla
¾ cup diced apple
¾ cup cranberries
½ cup raisins

Preheat oven to 350°. Grease muffin cups or use paper cups. Break egg into a mixing bowl; add sugar and whisk until smooth. Whisk in margarine and vanilla. Stir in fruit. Fold in dry ingredients until just moistened. Spoon batter into muffin cups. Bake 20-25 minutes, or until brown and firm to the touch. Do not freeze.

Brunetta Pfaender   *12 servings*

To check baking powder for freshness, put ½ teaspoon powder in a small bowl, and pour ¼ cup hot water over it. If the mixture bubbles, it is still good.

PUMPKIN MUFFINS

2 ¾ cups whole wheat flour
1 ½ teaspoons wheat germ
1 teaspoon baking soda
½ teaspoon ground cloves
¾ teaspoon cinnamon
½ teaspoon nutmeg
1 cup honey
4 large eggs
1 ½ cups canned pumpkin
1 cup vegetable oil
1 ½ cups raisins
1 cup walnuts

Preheat oven to 350°. Combine all dry ingredients, except raisins and walnuts. Mix together cooked pumpkin, eggs, honey and oil. Add dry ingredients. Stir mixture until lumps are gone. Fold in raisins and walnuts. Lightly coat muffin tins with oil and flour. Fill tins with mixture to ¾ full. Bake 15-20 minutes until brown and toothpick comes out clean.

Lillian Irene Preston   *24 servings*

 To prepare fresh pumpkin for use in cooking, first wash the pumpkin and dry. Cut into half, removing stem. Scrape out all stringy fiber and seeds. Place halves, cut side down, on a baking sheet. Bake at 325° about an hour, or until fork tender. Scrape pumpkin pulp from shells and run through a food processor, blender or food mill.

SOUR CREAM BISCUITS

    2 cups self-rising flour
    2 sticks butter or margarine
    1 (8 ounce) carton sour cream

Mix ingredients and drop into small muffin tins. Bake in a 400° oven for 12-15 minutes. Do not grease tins, or serve butter. So simple - so good!

Wilda Charlette

GRANDMOTHER JESSE'S RIZ BISCUITS

    1 package active dry yeast
    ¼ cup warm water
 2 ½ cups sifted flour
    1 tablespoon sugar
    ½ teaspoon baking soda
    1 teaspoon salt
    3 tablespoons butter or other shortening
    ½ cup lukewarm buttermilk

Dissolve yeast in water. Sift together flour, sugar, baking soda and salt into a bowl. Cut in shortening. Stir in buttermilk and dissolved yeast. Round up on floured board. Knead lightly. Roll out ¼ inch thick. Cut with a 2 inch biscuit cutter. Brush with melted butter. Let rise until doubled in size, about 45 minutes to an hour. Bake in a 400° oven for 10-12 minutes.

Julia Spitz   *about 18 biscuits*

PRALINE BISCUITS

½ cup butter
½ cup packed brown sugar
36 pecan halves or walnut halves
   cinnamon
   cloves
   nutmeg
2 cups biscuit making mix
½ cup applesauce
⅓ cup milk

Place 2 teaspoons of butter, approximately 1 tablespoon of brown sugar and 3 pecan halves in each of 12 muffin cups (regular muffin pan). Sprinkle cinnamon, cloves and nutmeg in each cup. Heat in oven until butter melts. Mix biscuit mix, applesauce and milk until dough forms. Spoon into muffin cups. Bake in a 450° oven 10 minutes. Take out of oven, invert immediately and cool.

Hint: This is excellent served for breakfast as well as a sweet snack after dinner.

Donna Peacock

 For variety, make biscuit sticks. Prepare any recipe for rolled biscuit dough. Cut the dough into sticks measuring ½x½x3 inches. Brush the sticks with melted butter and then bake accordingly to recipe instructions.

VIRGINIA BUTTERMILK BISCUITS

    2   cups flour
    2   teaspoons baking powder
    1   teaspoon salt
    ⅓   cup butter or other shortening
    ½   teaspoon baking soda
    1   cup buttermilk

Sift together flour, baking powder, sugar and salt into a medium-sized bowl. Cut in shortening with a fork until mixture looks like coarse meal. Dissolve baking soda in buttermilk and pour evenly over flour mixture, stirring until dry ingredients are moistened. Turn dough out onto a floured surface and knead 10-12 times. Roll out dough ½ inch thick. Cut with a 2 inch biscuit cutter. Place biscuits on a greased cookie sheet. Bake in a 450° oven for 10 minutes or until lightly browned.

KING ARTHUR POPOVERS

    2   eggs
    1   cup flour
    1   cup milk
    ½   teaspoon salt

Preheat oven to 425°. Mix all ingredients together until blended well. Grease a medium size muffin tin and fill each cup half full with batter. Bake about 25 minutes.

Shari Cromar   *12 servings*

PARKER HOUSE ROLLS

- 2 tablespoons butter or other shortening
- 1 teaspoon salt
- ¼ cup sugar
- 1 yeast cake
- 1 ½ cups lukewarm water
- 3 ½ cups sifted flour
- 1 egg, beaten well

Add butter, salt, sugar and crumbled yeast cake to water. Stir until butter is melted. Stir in sifted flour, cover and set in a warm place, free from drafts, to rise. (Dough may be set into unheated oven with a pan of hot water on lower shelf.) When double in bulk, add one egg. Knead lightly and let rise again to double in bulk. Roll out ½ inch thick on a floured board. Cut with a 2 inch biscuit cutter, crease in center with a dull knife. Brush with melted butter or other shortening and fold over, pinching the dough at sides to make a pocketbook. Brush tops with melted butter. Let rise and bake on a cookie sheet in a 400° oven about 20 minutes.

Margaret Carner   *2 dozen rolls*

 One package of dry yeast is equal to one yeast cake. Cake yeast can be refrigerated for up to two weeks in a tightly closed plastic bag. Dry yeast will keep for weeks outside the refrigerator and indefinitely inside.

GRANDMOTHER SPITZ'S REFRIGERATOR ROLLS

¾ cup sugar
1 cup shortening
2 tablespoons salt
1 cup boiling water
2 eggs, beaten
2 packages yeast
1 cup lukewarm water
6 cups flour
    melted butter to dip rolls in before putting in pan

Place sugar, shortening and salt into a large mixing bowl. Pour 1 cup boiling water over sugar mixture. Stir well. Cool to lukewarm. Stir in eggs. Set aside. Sprinkle yeast over 1 cup lukewarm water. Let stand for 5 minutes. Stir well and add to sugar mixture. Add flour and mix well. Put in refrigerator for 2 hours or knead until dough is easy to handle. (It will keep 4 or 5 days in the refrigerator.) Make dough into rolls or loaf. Cover and let rise until dough doubles in size. Bake in preheated 400° oven for 15 minutes or until golden brown.

 To "proof" yeast, add one teaspoon of sugar to the yeast-warm water mixture from the recipe. If the mixture bubbles up fairly quickly, the yeast is good.

SAUSAGE ROLLS

  2 cups all-purpose flour
  ½ teaspoon salt
  3 teaspoons baking powder
  7 tablespoons shortening
  ⅔ cup milk
  1 pound hot or medium sausage

Mix together flour, salt, baking powder, shortening and milk as for biscuits. Divide dough into two parts. Roll one part ¼ inch thick. With knife, spread ½ of sausage over the dough. Roll as for jelly roll. Repeat with remaining dough. Wrap in waxed paper and freeze. (It will keep indefinitely). When ready to use, slice ½ inch thick. Bake on rack of boiler pan in a 400° oven for 30 minutes or until golden brown. Serve immediately.

Wilda Charlette

MONKEY BREAD

  2 large cans of refrigerated biscuits
  ¾ cup butter or other shortening
  ½ cup brown sugar
    cinnamon to taste
  1 cup raisins or nuts

Preheat oven to 350°. Melt butter or other shortening. Quarter each biscuit and roll into a ball. Roll each piece through butter and brown sugar. Make layers on top of one another in pan. Sprinkle cinnamon and raisins/nuts on top of each layer. Repeat until dough balls and all ingredients are used. Bake for 30 minutes or until done.

Nancy Sutton   *makes 1 loaf*

ZUCCHINI BREAD

    2 cups grated zucchini
    3 eggs
    2 cups sugar
    1 cup oil
    3 cups flour
    1 teaspoon baking soda
    1 teaspoon salt
    ½ teaspoon baking powder
    2 teaspoons cinnamon
    ½ cup nuts
    3 teaspoons vanilla

Mix eggs, sugar and oil well. Add flour, baking soda, salt, baking powder, cinnamon, zucchini, nuts and vanilla, mixing well. Grease and flour 2 loaf pans. Bake in a 350° oven for 1 hour or until toothpick inserted into loaf comes out clean. Freezes well.

Sally Baker   *makes 2 loaves*

Bread should be thoroughly cooled before placing in a plastic bag or in foil. When freezing bread, be sure that all excess air is removed and the package is sealed tightly to avoid freezer burn.

APRICOT BREAD

  1 cup dried apricots, cut into small pieces
  2 cups warm water
  1 cup sugar
  2 tablespoons butter or other shortening
  1 egg
  ¾ cup orange juice
  2 cups all-purpose flour
  2 teaspoons baking powder
  ¼ teaspoon baking soda
  1 teaspoon salt
  ¾ cup chopped nuts

Soak apricots in 2 cups warm water for 30 minutes. Meanwhile, mix together sugar, butter or other shortening and egg. Stir in orange juice. In a separate bowl, combine flour, baking powder, salt and baking soda. Stir flour mixture into sugar mixture until combined. Drain apricots well, then add to batter along with nuts. Pour into a greased 9x5 inch loaf pan. Bake in a 350° oven for 55 minutes or until done. Cool in pan 10 minutes before turning on rack.

GLAZE
  2 tablespoons orange juice
  2 tablespoons sugar

Heat and pour over loaf, if desired.

Wilda Charlette   *makes 1 loaf*

BANANA BREAD

    1   stick butter, softened
    1   cup sugar
    2   medium or 1 large egg
    1   tablespoon vanilla extract
    1   teaspoon rum extract
    1   teaspoon baking soda
    1   teaspoon baking powder
    ½   teaspoon salt
    ½   cup chopped nuts
    3   very ripe bananas, mashed
    2   cups flour

Preheat oven to 350°. Blend butter and sugar. Add eggs and extracts. Sift together flour, baking soda, baking powder and salt. Blend all together. Add bananas and nuts. Bake for 1 hour or until toothpick comes out clean. Optional: add any of the following ingredients, ½ cup raisins, dates, coconut, or chocolate chips. For cupcakes, bake 25 minutes.

Gail Hill-Smith   *makes 2 loaves*

Peel and mash overripe bananas, adding a little lemon juice. Freeze in measured amounts. Thaw as needed for use in making banana cake, bread or muffins.

CRANBERRY FRUIT AND NUT BREAD

  1   cup cranberries
  ½ cup chopped nuts
  1   tablespoon grated orange peel
  1   cup orange juice
  1   egg, well beaten
  1   cup all-purpose flour
  1   cup wheat flour
  ½ cup sugar
  ½ cup brown sugar
1 ½ teaspoons baking powder
  1   teaspoon salt
  ½ teaspoon baking soda
  2   tablespoons shortening

Preheat oven to 350°. Grease and flour a 9x5x3 inch loaf pan. Combine cranberries, nuts, orange peel, orange juice and egg. In another bowl, combine flours, sugars, baking powder, salt and baking soda. Cut in shortening. Fold in wet ingredients. Spoon into pan and bake for 1 hour.

Carla Reid   *makes 1 loaf*

When using fresh oranges or lemons for juice, first grate the rind. It freezes well for later use.

DATE AND NUT LOAF

1   cup sugar
1   cup flour
4   egg yolks, separated
1   teaspoon baking powder
½   cup brandy or pineapple juice
1   teaspoon vanilla
1   pound pitted dates (whole)
1   pound English walnuts (pieces as large as possible)
½   pound Brazil nuts (whole) (easier to shell if frozen first)
½   pound candied cherries (whole)

In a large bowl, mix sugar, flour, egg yolks, baking powder, brandy or pineapple juice and vanilla. Beat egg whites until fairly stiff and add to flour mixture. Pour mixture over fruit and nuts. Line pan with buttered wax paper. Bake in a 300° oven for 1 hour. Cut with a sharp knife.

Donalda Easterbrook   *makes 2 loaves*

Nut and fruit breads may be baked in 6 ounce fruit juice cans, so that they can be cut into decorative small slices. Do not fill the cans more than ¾ full to allow for expansion of the dough.

STRAWBERRY NUT BREAD

  1 (10 ounce) package sliced frozen strawberries, drained
  2 eggs
  ½ cup vegetable oil
  1 cup sugar
  2 cups unsifted all-purpose flour
1 ½ teaspoons cinnamon
  1 teaspoon baking powder
  1 teaspoon baking soda
  ½ teaspoon nutmeg
  ½ teaspoon salt
  ¾ cup chopped pecans

Preheat oven to 350°. Defrost strawberries according to package instructions. Beat eggs until fluffy. Add oil, sugar and strawberries, beating until light. Mix flour, cinnamon, baking powder, baking soda,
nutmeg and salt. Blend flour mixture into strawberry mixture until
moistened. Do not over mix. Stir in nuts. Pour into a greased 9x5 inch
loaf pan. Bake at for 50-60 minutes or until toothpick inserted in center comes out clean. Cool 5 minutes and remove from pan. Finish cooling on rack.

Mary Stewart   *12 servings*

EASY CHEESE BREAD

  1 egg, beaten
  ½ cup milk
1 ½ cups biscuit making mix
  2 cups grated cheese

Preheat oven to 400°. Combine egg, milk, biscuit mix and 1 cup of
cheese. Pour into a greased 8x4x3 inch loaf pan. Sprinkle with remaining cheese. Bake 20 minutes.

Julia Spitz   *makes 1 loaf*

ONION CHEESE SUPPER BREAD

　½　cup chopped onion
　1　egg, beaten
　½　cup milk
1 ½　cups biscuit making mix
　1　cup shredded sharp cheddar cheese
　2　tablespoons snipped parsley
　2　tablespoons melted butter

Cook onion in small amount of butter until tender, not brown. Combine egg and milk. Add biscuit mix. Stir only until moistened. Add onion, parsley and ½ cup of the cheese. Spread dough into a greased 8x1 ½ inch round cake pan. Sprinkle with remaining cheese. Drizzle melted butter over top. Bake in a 400° oven for 20 minutes or until a toothpick inserted in bread comes out clean.

Linda Tinsley

CLAM FRITTERS

24　soft clams
　2　cups flour
　2　teaspoons baking powder
　½　teaspoon salt
　1　cup milk
　½　cup clam liquor
　2　eggs, well beaten
　　salt and pepper

Mix flour, baking powder, salt, milk, clam liquor and eggs. Chop clams and season with salt and pepper. Add to batter. Stir. Drop by tablespoonfuls into deep, hot fat (360°-370°). Fry 2-3 minutes.

Margaret Carner　　　　　　　　　　　　　　　*4 to 6 servings*

Cheese
&
Eggs

St. John's Episcopal Church

St. John's Episcopal Church was established in 1829 and the present building was built in 1880 in the Gothic Revival style after a fire destroyed the first church. Interesting features of the building made with hand-hewn pine timbers and locally made bricks include a system of beams and trusses in an open ceiling which resembles the inverted hull of a ship; granite sills which came from Andrew Jackson's arsenal at Chattahoochee; stained glass windows; and the altar and reredos which is hand carved from six different kinds of wood - magnolia, oak, pine, cherry, walnut, and torreya. The bell tower contains a 14-bell carillon, one of a few in this country which is still rung by hand. A garden behind the church offers a place for quiet rest or meditation.

EASY CHEESY BRUNCH CASSEROLE

      4   slices white bread
      1   medium onion, chopped
      1   cup fresh mushrooms, sliced
      2   tablespoons butter or margarine, melted
      8   slices of bacon, cooked
      1   cup cooked ham, chopped
      1   cup (4 ounces) cheddar cheese, shredded
      1   cup (4 ounces) Swiss cheese, shredded
      1   tablespoon all-purpose flour
   1 ¼   cups milk
      4   large eggs, beaten
      1   tablespoon prepared mustard
      ½   teaspoon garlic salt

Place bread slices in the bottom of a lightly greased 8 inch square baking dish. Set aside. Sauté onion and mushrooms in butter until tender. Spoon evenly over bread. Top with ham and bacon. Combine cheese and flour, then sprinkle over ham and bacon. Combine milk, eggs, mustard and garlic salt. Pour over cheese. Cover and chill 8 hours. Remove from refrigerator and let stand 30 minutes. Bake uncovered in a 375° oven for 35 minutes or until set. Let stand 10 minutes before serving.

Tammy Barkve   *4 to 6 servings*

NEW ENGLAND CHEESE PUFFS

1 cup sifted flour
1 teaspoon baking powder
½ teaspoon salt
¼ teaspoon paprika
¼ teaspoon dry mustard
2 eggs, separated
½ cup milk
1 cup American cheese, grated

Sift dry ingredients together in a bowl. Beat yolks of eggs and add to milk. Stir into dry ingredients and mix well. Add cheese. Beat egg whites until stiff and fold into the batter. Drop by spoonfuls into hot, deep fat (360°). Cook until a golden brown. Drain on paper towel before serving.

6 servings

CHEESE GRITS WITH SAUSAGE

1 pound bulk sausage
1 roll garlic cheese
1 stick butter or margarine
1 cup quick grits
2 eggs
   milk

Brown sausage well and drain. Set aside. Cook grits and add butter and cheese. Beat eggs in a measuring cup, adding enough milk to make one cup. Add egg mixture to grits. Mix together grits and sausage in a 2 quart casserole. Bake in a 350° oven for 1 hour.

Ginger Phillips   *6 to 8 servings*

CHILE CHEESE GRITS

1 ½ cups uncooked grits
3 eggs, beaten
1 pound Colby Jack cheese, shredded
½ cup butter or margarine
1 (4 ounce) can chopped green chilies, undrained
1 tablespoon seasoning salt
¼ teaspoon hot sauce
¼ teaspoon paprika
¼ teaspoon Worcestershire sauce

Cook grits in a large saucepan according to package directions. Add eggs, cheese, butter, green chilies, seasoning salt, hot sauce, paprika and Worcestershire sauce. Stir well until cheese and butter begin to melt. Pour grits mixture into a 13x9x2 inch baking pan. Bake in a 250° oven for 1 ½ hours or until set. Serve warm.

Sandi Bridwell   *12 servings*

STUFFED EGGS SOPHISTICATE

12 hard-cooked eggs
1 (3 ounce) package cream cheese, softened
½ cup sour cream
2 tablespoons melted butter
¼ teaspoon Tabasco sauce
¾ -1 teaspoon salt
¼ teaspoon dry mustard

Cut eggs lengthwise into quarters and remove egg yolk, leaving egg whites intact. Put egg yolks through a sieve and set aside. Beat cream cheese until fluffy; blend in sour cream, butter, Tabasco sauce, salt and mustard. Add egg yolks, mixing lightly. Fill egg whites (mixture can be piped through a pastry bag and tube). Sprinkle with paprika.

Inez B. Dasher   *8 servings*

EGGS PONCE DE LEON

      6 hard-cooked eggs
    ½ onion, diced
      1 tablespoon butter
      1 tablespoon flour
      2 cups tomato juice
    ½ cup chopped celery
    ¼ cup chopped green pepper
    ½ cup mushrooms
         salt and pepper to taste
    ½ teaspoon Worcestershire sauce
    ½ cup Thin White Sauce
         cracker crumbs

Chop whites of eggs and mash yolks. Brown onion in butter, add flour and blend. Add tomato juice, celery and green pepper and bring to a boil, stirring constantly. Simmer until celery and pepper are tender. Add mushrooms, seasoning and Worcestershire sauce. Blend well. Add white sauce, egg whites and egg yolks. Place in a buttered casserole dish. Sprinkle with cracker crumbs, dot with butter and brown in a 400° oven.   Serve hot.

THIN WHITE SAUCE
      1 tablespoon butter
      1 tablespoon flour
    ½ teaspoon salt
    ⅛ teaspoon pepper
      1 cup milk

Melt butter and blend in flour, salt and pepper. Add milk gradually, stirring constantly until mixture boils and thickens, then cook 2-3 minutes longer. Place over hot water to keep warm and cover tightly to prevent film from forming.

Margaret Carner   *6 servings*

HERB AND NUT OMELET

4 tablespoons butter
6 scallions, finely chopped
2 lettuce leaves, finely chopped
1 teaspoon dried dill (or 3 tablespoons fresh dill weed)
¼ cup chopped parsley
8 eggs
¼ teaspoon turmeric
  pinch of cinnamon
  salt and pepper to taste
¼ cup raisins, chopped
¼ cup walnuts, chopped

Melt 2 tablespoons butter in an iron skillet. Add scallions, dill and parsley and sauté until the scallions are transparent. Add the remaining 2 tablespoons butter and melt. Preheat oven to 350°. Beat eggs well and add turmeric, cinnamon, salt and pepper. Stir in raisins and nuts. Add this mixture to the skillet but do not stir. Transfer skillet to preheated oven and bake until golden and set. Serve immediately.

4 servings

 Large eggs are the standard size used in most recipes. Be sure to adjust the number of eggs accordingly if using a different size.

NANCY'S SPINACH QUICHE

1 (10 ounce) package frozen spinach
1 (3 ounce) package cream cheese, softened
1 cup shredded sharp cheddar cheese
5 eggs, slightly beaten
½ teaspoon salt
¼ cup chopped green onion
2 teaspoons chopped parsley
1 unbaked 9 inch pastry shell
1 ripe tomato (thinly sliced)
¼ cup Parmesan cheese

Cook spinach; drain and squeeze out water. Combine cream cheese, cheddar cheese, eggs, salt, green onion and parsley. Beat lightly with a fork. Stir in spinach and pour into pastry shell. Arrange sliced tomatoes on top. Sprinkle with Parmesan cheese. Bake in a 425° oven for 35 minutes or until slightly brown on top.

Nancy Sutton   *4 to 6 servings*

 Quiche is traditionally served lukewarm, so time your food preparation accordingly.

MUSHROOM QUICHE

1	9 inch unbaked pie shell
2	tablespoons minced green onion
2	tablespoons butter or margarine
½	pound fresh mushrooms, cleaned and sliced
½	teaspoon lemon juice
½	teaspoon salt
3	eggs, beaten
1 ½	cups heavy cream
	pepper to taste
1	cup shredded (4 ounces) Swiss cheese

Preheat oven to 375°. In a medium size skillet, sauté onion in butter for 2 minutes. Add mushrooms, lemon juice and salt. Sauté until liquid evaporates. Set aside. In a large mixing bowl thoroughly combine eggs, cream and pepper. Slowly stir in mushroom mixture and cheese. Pour into pie shell. Bake 30-35 minutes or until knife inserted 1 inch from edge comes out clean. Let stand 15 minutes before serving.

Martha Eacker   *4 to 6 servings*

Buy mushrooms past their prime (when the prices can be real bargains). Slice, sauté in butter and freeze in recipe-sized packages. When added to dishes being cooked, they will taste as good as fresh.

WILD RICE AND MUSHROOM QUICHE

      4   slices bacon
      ⅔   cup wild rice, uncooked
      2   cups water
  1 ½   cups shredded Swiss cheese (6 ounce)
      ½   cup finely chopped green onions
      1   cup fresh mushrooms, chopped
      1   cup tomatoes, peeled, chopped and drained
           salt and pepper to taste
      4   large eggs
      2   cups whipping cream
    16   3 inch frozen pastry shells, unbaked, OR
      2   9 inch pastry-lined quiche dishes

Cook bacon in large skillet until crisp; remove and crumble bacon, reserving 1 tablespoon drippings. Combine rice, water, and bacon drippings in a heavy saucepan. Bring to a boil, cover, reduce heat and simmer 50-60 minutes or until tender. Drain excess liquid (if any). Combine cooked rice, bacon, cheese, onions, mushrooms, tomatoes, salt and pepper; set aside. Combine eggs and whipping cream in large bowl, beat at high speed with electric mixer for 2 minutes. Stir in rice mixture. Spoon into pastry shells or quiche dish. Place pastry shells on baking sheet, bake 375° for 25-30 minutes. If using quiche dishes, bake in a 375° oven on lower rack of oven for 45 minutes, covering loosely with foil to prevent excessive browning.

16 servings

SEAFOOD QUICHE WITH RICE CRUST

8 ounces cooked shrimp or crab meat
½ cup finely chopped onion
¼ cup fresh parsley, chopped
1 garlic clove, minced
4 ounces part skim mozzarella or Swiss cheese, grated
1 cup low-fat cottage cheese
1 cup egg beaters
2 tablespoons black pepper
2 tablespoons grated Parmesan or Romano cheese
cooking spray

BROWN RICE CRUST: Combine 1 ½ cups cooked brown rice, 2 tablespoons grated Parmesan cheese and 2 egg whites. Pat rice evenly into a 9 inch pie pan sprayed with cooking spray.

Combine remaining ingredients except Parmesan or Romano cheese. Mix well and pour into prepared rice crust. Top with grated Parmesan or Romano cheese. Bake in a 375° oven for 40-45 minutes.

Debi Barrett-Hayes   *6 servings*

Canned shrimp lose their "canned" taste after soaking in two tablespoons of vinegar and a teaspoon of sherry for fifteen minutes.

EGG AND SAUSAGE QUICHE

   1   unbaked 9 inch pie crust or 9 ⅝ inch pie shell
   1   pound ground sausage
   1   medium size onion, chopped
   4   eggs, beaten
1 ½   cups evaporated milk
  ½   teaspoon seasoning salt
       dash of red pepper or paprika
   2   cups cheese (can be cheddar, Swiss, Monterey Jack), grated
   2   tablespoons flour

Preheat oven to 350°. Beat eggs, milk and seasonings together. Set aside. Brown sausage and onions. Drain. Mix flour with cheese. Place sausage and onion mixture into pie shell. Add cheese mixture. Pour eggs over sausage and cheese. Bake 40-45 minutes. Let stand for 10 minutes before serving.

Variation: 1 pound link sausage, cut in ½ inch pieces, browned and drained, can be substituted for ground sausage.

Donna Peacock   *8 servings*

 Cheddar, Swiss and other hard cheeses can be shredded more easily if they are first chilled in the freezer for 15 minutes.

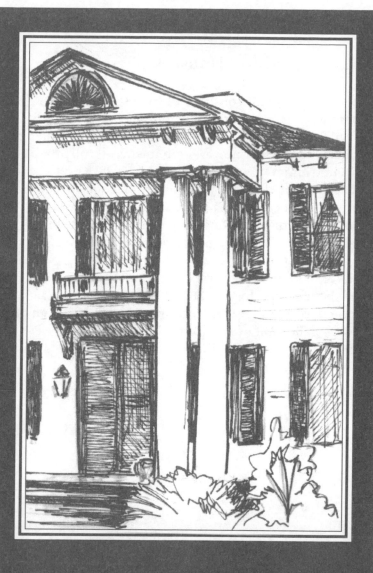

Entrees

Knott House Museum

Since its original construction in 1843, the Knott House has been home to changing social, economic, and political life in Tallahassee. William Valentine Knott, who served as Florida's treasurer, comptroller, and first auditor, and ran unsuccessfully for governor in 1916, acquired and remodeled the house in 1928. Knott's wife, Luella, was an accomplished musician, poet, and leader in the Temperance Movement. Luella composed whimsical poems about the Victorian era furnishings in the home and tied them with satin ribbons to many pieces of furniture, Thus, the house became affectionately known as "The House That Rhymes."

The Knott House, its furnishings, and the family's personal effects were bequeathed to the State of Florida in 1986. The home has been restored to its 1928 appearance and is now a museum filled with a marvelous collection of antiques. The rooms remain as they were when the Knott family resided in it and provide a glimpse of Tallahassee's social, economic, and political history.

CRESCENT BEEF ROLL

½ pound ground beef
½ onion, chopped
1 teaspoon salt
½ teaspoon pepper
2 tablespoons ketchup or barbecue sauce
1 (8 count) package refrigerated crescent rolls

Preheat oven to 350°. Sauté onion (do not brown); add ground beef, salt, pepper and ketchup or barbecue sauce. Cook until beef is brown. Open package of crescent rolls and stretch them as much as possible. Place 4 crescent rolls flat on a greased or Teflon cookie sheet. Fill each roll with meat mixture. Place another flat roll on top of this; with a fork, press down all the edges of the crescent roll to seal in the meat mixture. Bake until brown (approximately 15 minutes).

Mrs. Joseph A Boyd, Jr.   *4 servings*

HAMBURGER PIE

1 pound lean ground beef
2 ⅔ cups mashed potato flakes
1 egg
1 teaspoon salt (optional)
⅛ teaspoon pepper
1 tablespoon minced onion
¼ cup ketchup
1 cup milk
½ cup shredded cheese (optional)

Preheat oven to 350°. Mix together meat, 1 ⅓ cup dry potatoes and the next 6 ingredients. Pat into an ungreased pie pan. Bake, uncovered, for 35-40 minutes. Prepare remaining potatoes according to package direction for a 4 serving amount. Spread on top of baked pie. Top with cheese and return to oven until cheese melts.

Kim Cooper   *4 to 6 servings*

WAIKIKI MEATBALLS

1 ½   pounds ground beef
⅔   cup cracker crumbs
⅓   cup minced onion
1   egg
1 ½   teaspoons salt
¼   teaspoon ginger
¼   cup milk
1   tablespoon shortening
2   tablespoons cornstarch
½   cup brown sugar (packed)
1   (13 ½ ounce) can pineapple tidbits, drained (reserve syrup)
⅓   cup vinegar
1   tablespoon soy sauce
⅓   cup chopped green pepper

Thoroughly mix together ground beef, crumbs, onion, egg, salt, ginger and milk. Shape mixture by rounded tablespoonfuls into balls. Melt shortening in a large skillet; brown meatballs. Remove meatballs; keep warm. Pour fat from skillet. Mix cornstarch and sugar. Stir in reserved pineapple syrup, vinegar and soy sauce until smooth. Pour into skillet; cook over medium heat, stirring constantly, until mixture thickens and boils. Boil 1 minute, stirring frequently. Add meatballs, pineapple tidbits and green pepper; heat thoroughly.

Serving Suggestion: May be served over rice or couscous. Also makes a good appetizer.

Tammy Brizzi   *6 servings*

NEAPOLITAN MEATLOAF

1   pound ground chuck
1   pound ground mild Italian sausage
2   egg whites
1   large slice white bread soaked in milk
1   tablespoon salt
1   tablespoon finely ground fennel seeds
½   cup ketchup
1   tablespoon mustard
1   tablespoon Parmesan cheese
1   tablespoon basil leaves
1   teaspoon oregano
1   teaspoon ground pepper
1   (10 ounce) can whole tomatoes
1   large onion, chopped

Mix ground chuck with sausage, bread (squeeze milk from the bread before adding to meat) and egg whites. Add remaining ingredients except tomatoes and onion. Shape into an oblong loaf. Place meatloaf in a greased 9x5x3 inch pan. Mix tomatoes and onions and pour over meatloaf. Bake in a 350° oven for 1 hour.

Serving Suggestion: Leftover meatloaf makes excellent sandwiches, either hot or cold.

Anne Core   *6 servings*

CAPE COD CRANBERRY MEATLOAF

¾   cup whole cranberry sauce
¾   cup dark brown sugar
1   pound ground chuck
1   pound ground veal
½   pound ground pork
1   medium onion, finely chopped
½   cup milk
½   cup dry bread crumbs
¼   cup ketchup
2   eggs
½   teaspoon each thyme, marjoram, rosemary
¼   teaspoon ground white pepper
1   teaspoon salt
2   whole bay leaves

Preheat oven to 350°. Combine cranberry sauce and brown sugar in the bottom of a 9x5x3 inch loaf pan. In a large bowl, combine remaining ingredients, except for bay leaves and mix well. Shape into a loaf and place over sauce. Top with bay leaves and bake 1 ¼ -1 ½ hours. Remove bay leaves and transfer meatloaf to a serving platter. Drizzle pan juices, especially the cranberries, over the loaf before serving.

Diane Mahlert   *4 to 6 servings*

To make bread crumbs, place toasted white bread (or crusts) in blender or food processor. Store covered in refrigerator or freezer. To make soft or untoasted bread crumbs, slice bread thinly and allow to air dry for a few hours before blending.

MARINATED BEEF TENDERLOIN

  1 (5 pound) beef tenderloin, trimmed

MARINADE
  ½ cup Burgundy wine
  ¼ cup olive oil
  ¼ cup soy sauce
  1 tablespoon dried parsley
  1 tablespoon paprika
1 ½ tablespoons seasoned salt
  ⅓ cup tarragon, minced

GARNISH
     endive
     cherry tomatoes

Combine marinade ingredients and mix well. Place trimmed tenderloin in a large baking dish. Pour marinade over and cover tightly. Refrigerate at least 2 hours; turning twice. Uncover tenderloin and place dish on bottom rack of oven (do not drain). Broil for 20 minutes on each side. Cover and bake in a 350° oven for 10-15 minutes. Garnish and slice to serve.

Geogianna Wollschlager   *8 to 10 servings*

 If you will be starting with frozen meat, you can place marinade and frozen meat in a sealed plastic bag. Let thaw in the refrigerator, turning the bag several times.

BEEF AND BROCCOLI

  1   pound beef flank or sirloin steak
1 ½ pounds broccoli
  ½   pound fresh mushrooms, sliced
  ¼   cup onion, thinly sliced
  2   tablespoons olive oil

SAUCE
  ¼   cup chicken broth
  ⅓   cup soy sauce
  1   tablespoon vodka
  2   tablespoons dry sherry
  1   teaspoon ground ginger
  2   tablespoons cornstarch
  ¼   cup water

Mix sauce ingredients in a bowl and set aside. Partially freeze beef and slice very thinly on the diagonal. Slice broccoli stems about ¼ inch thick and separate florets into small pieces. In a wok, heat olive oil until very hot, but not smoking. Stir fry beef slices for 1 minute. Add broccoli stems and stir fry for 1 minute. Add florets, onions and mushrooms and cook for 3 minutes. Stir in sauce; mix and cook until thickened. Serve over rice.

Julie Blankenship

To stir fry, first chop food into small uniform pieces. Cook small amounts at a time quickly in hot oil over high heat, tossing and turning constantly.

BRAZILIAN POT ROAST

      4   pounds chuck roast, trimmed of fat
    ¼   cup cooking oil
      1   tablespoon dry mustard
    ½   tablespoon salt
    ½   teaspoon pepper
      1   cup sliced onion
  1 ½   tablespoons brown sugar
    ¼   cup vinegar
    ½   cup water
      9   red potatoes, peeled and halved
  1 ½   cups sliced carrots

Brown roast in hot oil in a heavy pot for ½ hour, uncovered. Add seasonings, sugar, onion, ½ cup water and vinegar. Cover and simmer slowly for 3 ½ hours. One hour before serving, add potatoes and carrots to broth. Cover and continue to simmer for 1 hour. Remove from heat and let stand for 15 minutes before serving.

Julie Blankenship   *6 servings*

EASY RIBS

  1 ¾   pounds lean spareribs (cut in ½ lengthwise)
      2   tablespoons cooking oil
           pinch of salt
      2   tablespoons brown sugar
    ¼   cup soy sauce or Worcestershire sauce

Heat oil in frying pan. Fry ribs until meat color has just changed from pink to gray. Add salt, sugar and sauce; mix well. Pour enough water over ribs to barely cover. Keep uncovered and bring to a boil, stirring occasionally. When liquid thickens, stir constantly (approximately ½ hour) until ribs are well glazed and almost no liquid is left.

Ann Boyd   *4 servings*

SECRET RIBS

    2   racks of ribs, split lengthwise and cracked
    2   teaspoons marjoram, finely crushed
 2 ½   teaspoons sweet basil, finely crushed
    1   teaspoon oregano, finely crushed
    4   tablespoons Worcestershire sauce
         juice of 1 lime (about ¼ cup)
         pepper to taste

Wash ribs in cool water and blot dry with paper towels; place in an aluminum foil lined broiler pan. Sprinkle seasonings over meat; pepper meat as desired. Pour sauce and lime juice over meat. Pour ¼ cup of water in bottom of 11x17 inch broiler pan. Steam meat in a 300° oven for 20-30 minutes. Finish cooking ribs on the grill until done.

6 to 8 servings

SWISS STEAK

    1   large round steak
    1   cup flour
    1   teaspoon salt
    3   teaspoons garlic powder
    2   (16 ounce) cans stewed tomatoes
    1   large onion, chopped
    1   green pepper, chopped

Tenderize round steak by hammering. Mix flour, salt and garlic powder. Bread steak with flour mixture, pressing into steak well. In a frying pan, brown on both sides. Combine stewed tomatoes, onion and green pepper. Pour ½ of mixture into 12x9 inch pan. Place steak in pan. Pour remaining mixture on top. Cover with aluminum foil and bake in a 350° oven for 23 minutes per pound.

Mimi Reina   *4 servings*

FESTIVE FAJITAS

1   pound beef round steak or 2 whole chicken breasts,
    cut into thin strips
2   tablespoons oil
1   medium green pepper, cut into strips
1   medium onion, sliced
4   ounces mild Mexican pasteurized processed cheese spread
4   8 inch flour tortillas
1   cup chopped tomato

In a large skillet, sauté meat in oil for 4 minutes. Add peppers and onions; mix lightly. Reduce heat to medium. Cook 5 minutes or until steak is tender or chicken is done; drain. Add cheese; stir until melted. Fill tortillas with meat mixture and tomatoes.

Microwave: Reduce oil to 1 tablespoon. Microwave meat and oil in a 1 ½ quart microwave-safe bowl on HIGH 4-6 minutes, stirring after 3 minutes. Stir in peppers and onions. Microwave on HIGH 4-6 minutes or until vegetables are crisp-tender, stirring every 2 minutes. Add cheese. Microwave on HIGH 2-2 ½ minutes or until cheese is melted. Stir. Fill tortillas with meat mixture and tomatoes.

Tammy Barkve   *4 servings*

Boneless chicken breasts and other meats are much easier to slice thinly if almost frozen. If using fresh meat, freeze for 45 minutes or until it is almost firm to the touch.

FIESTA

       2   pounds ground round steak
       2   cups rice
      ½   cup milk
       1   can cheese soup
       2   packages chili seasoning
       1   cup water
           shredded lettuce
           grated sharp Cheddar cheese
           chopped tomatoes
           sliced black olives
           chopped pecans
           sour cream
           salsa
           corn chips

In a large skillet, brown the ground round, then drain. Add chili seasoning and 1 cup water. Cook rice in a separate pan. Add milk to cheese soup and cook on low. Serve on individual plates in layers as follows: corn chips, rice, ground round, cheese soup, shredded lettuce, grated cheese, chopped tomatoes, sliced olives, salsa, sour cream and chopped pecans.

Linda Clark   *6 servings*

LAMB SHANKS IN RED WINE

     4 strips bacon, chopped
     6 lamb shanks
     1 carrot, chopped
     1 medium onion, chopped
     1 garlic clove, minced
     1 celery stalk, chopped
 1 ½ teaspoons salt
     ½ teaspoon cracked pepper
     2 tablespoons flour
     1 cup beef broth
     1 cup dry red wine
     1 bay leaf
     ¼ teaspoon rosemary
   12 small pearl onions
   18 medium mushrooms

In a large pan, sauté bacon for 3 minutes. Add the lamb shanks and brown evenly. Remove bacon and shanks. Stir in chopped carrot, celery, onion and garlic. Season with salt and pepper. Sauté until the vegetables are soft. Stir in the flour, blending with the vegetables. Return the bacon and the lamb shanks to the casserole. Pour in the beef broth and wine. Add the bay leaf and rosemary. Cover and simmer on low for 1 hour. Add the pearl onions and simmer covered for 20 minutes. Add the mushrooms and simmer covered for 10 additional minutes.

Julie Blankenship   *6 servings*

LAMB STEW

2 ½   pounds boneless lamb, cut into 1 ½ inch pieces
⅓   cup all-purpose flour
2 ½   teaspoons salt
¼   teaspoon pepper
¼ -½   cup butter
1   medium onion, quartered
1   clove garlic, crushed
12   medium yellow or Vidalia onions, peeled
12   medium whole mushrooms
1   teaspoon sugar
1 ¼   teaspoons dried thyme
2   sprigs fresh parsley
1   large bay leaf
2   cups water
1 ½   cups red wine
1   pound small carrots
1 ¼   pounds small new potatoes (about 8 large)
  chopped parsley

Wipe lamb with damp paper towels. On wax paper combine flour, salt and pepper. Coat lamb evenly with mixture. Reserve leftover flour. In a heavy pan (Dutch Oven), brown lamb, quartered onion and garlic in hot butter. Drain lamb pieces on paper towels. Add onions, mushrooms and sugar to drippings in pan. Cook covered for 5 minutes or until lightly browned. Return lamb to Dutch Oven. Add thyme, parsley and bay leaf. Toss with drippings to coat evenly. Stir in 2 cups water and 1 cup wine. Place large sheet of waxed paper over top of Dutch oven and place lid on top of paper, letting paper hang over. Bring to boil. Reduce heat and simmer covered for 40 minutes. Pare a 1 inch band of skin from center of each potato and add carrots and potatoes to lamb. Stir to combine. Return to a boil. Reduce heat and simmer covered for 40 minutes or until meat and vegetables are tender. Remove from heat and skim fat from surface. Combine reserved flour mixture and ½ cup red wine. Stir into liquid in Dutch oven. Simmer covered 10 minutes or until slightly thickened. Remove from

(Continued on next page)

(Lamb Stew continued)

heat. Add a little more wine to thin sauce if necessary. Sprinkle with chopped parsley.

Julie Blankenship   *8 servings*

SPICY LEG OF LAMB

4-6 pound leg of lamb
2 tablespoons flour
1 teaspoon curry
⅛ teaspoon black pepper
⅛ teaspoon white pepper
½ teaspoon finely minced garlic
½ cup spicy mango chutney
¼ cup steak sauce
2 tablespoons ketchup
1 tablespoon wine vinegar
½ teaspoon Worcestershire sauce
   dash of hot sauce
¼ cup chopped scallions

Trim fat from lamb. Line a large cooking pan with aluminum foil. Place leg of lamb in pan. Mix together all dry ingredients except scallions and massage into lamb. Mix together chutney, garlic, steak sauce, catsup, wine vinegar, Worcestershire sauce and hot sauce. Pour over lamb. Sprinkle scallions over lamb. Seal lamb with another piece of foil, crimped at edges to the bottom sheet. Bake in a 350° oven for 35-40 minutes per pound. Roll the meat every 30 minutes.

Serving Suggestion: Serve with herbed or white rice.

Debi Barrett-Hayes   *4 to 6 servings*

PORK CHOPS IN TOMATO AND PEPPER SAUCE

      6   lean pork loin chops, boneless
     ¼   cup oil
      1   small onion, peeled and sliced
      1   green pepper, cleaned and sliced
      1   pound fresh mushrooms, sliced
      1   (16 ounce) can Italian style tomatoes, broken up with fork
      3   tablespoons tomato paste
     ⅔   cup red wine
   1 ½   tablespoons dried basil
      3   tablespoons butter
          garlic salt and pepper to taste
   1 ½   tablespoons cornstarch

Wash pork chops. Heat oil in a heavy skillet. Season pork chops with garlic salt and pepper and brown in oil. Remove chops and discard all but 3 tablespoons of drippings. Add basil and stir to mix with oil. Stir in the wine and bring to a boil. Stir in the tomatoes and tomato paste. Return the chops to the pan and coat with the tomato mixture. Cover and simmer 35-40 minutes, basting occasionally. Melt the butter in another pan. Add the peppers and onion and sauté until softened. Stir in the mushrooms and continue to sauté for 3 minutes. Stir the vegetables into the tomato mixture. Continue cooking until chops are tender. Transfer the chops to a serving platter. Stir 1 ½ tablespoons cornstarch into 2 tablespoons water. Stir the dissolved cornstarch into the sauce and simmer, stirring, until thickened. Pour sauce over chops and serve over rice.

Sharon Piepmeier   *6 servings*

SWEET-AND-SOUR PORK CHOPS

>   8   pork chops
>   1   can pie apples
>   3   small onions, sliced

SAUCE

>   1   cup ketchup
>   ¼   cup Worcestershire sauce
>   8   tablespoons light brown sugar
>   3   tablespoons cider vinegar

Remove fat from pork chops. Mix together ingredients for sauce. Line the bottom of a 9x13 inch glass or aluminum pan with onions and apples. Pour half of the sauce over onions and apples. Layer pork chops over sauce, then cover with remaining sauce. Cover and bake in a 350° oven for 1 hour. Uncover and bake for 30 more minutes.

Sally Baker   *4 to 8 servings*

PORK CHOP AND POTATO SCALLOP

>   4-6   pork chops
>   ½   cup sour cream (optional)
>   1   can cream of mushroom soup
>   ¼   cup water
>   4   cups sliced potatoes
>   salt and pepper

Season pork chops; brown in a skillet. Blend soup, sour cream and water. In a 9x13 inch casserole dish, alternate layers of potatoes (sprinkled with salt and pepper) and layers of soup mixture. Top with chops. Cover and bake in a 375° oven for 1 hour, 15 minutes.

Linda Tinsley   *4 to 6 servings*

BAKED CHOPS WITH VEGETABLES

 2 tablespoons olive oil
 6 (¾ inch thick) pork loin chops
 1 medium green pepper, chopped
 1 medium onion, chopped
 1 clove garlic, pressed
 1 cup chopped celery
 ¼ cup butter or margarine
 1 (8 ¾ ounce) can whole kernel corn, drained
 1 cup Italian style bread crumbs
 1 egg, beaten
 1 teaspoon seasoned salt
 ¼ teaspoon lemon pepper
 2 tablespoons butter or margarine
 3 tablespoons all-purpose flour
 1 cup milk

Heat oil in a large skillet over medium heat; add pork chops and brown on both sides. Remove chops from skillet and drain on paper towels; drain off pan drippings. Sauté green pepper, onion, celery and pressed garlic in ¼ cup butter in a medium saucepan. Remove from heat; add corn, bread crumbs, egg, salt and pepper, stirring until well blended. Set vegetable mix aside. Melt 2 tablespoons butter in a heavy saucepan over low heat; add flour, stirring until smooth. Cook 1 minute, stirring constantly. Gradually add milk; cook over medium heat, stirring constantly until thickened and bubbly. Arrange pork chops in a lightly greased 13x9x2 inch baking dish. Spoon vegetable mix over pork chops. Pour white sauce evenly over vegetable mix. Bake uncovered in a 300° oven for 45 minutes or until pork chops are tender. Serve immediately.

Sandi Bridwell   *6 servings*

PORK CHOPS WITH APPLES & BOURBON

4 boneless loin pork chops, cut 1 inch thick and trimmed of fat
1 clove of garlic, halved lengthwise
  pinch of sage
2 tablespoons margarine
¼ teaspoon hot sauce
1 teaspoon fresh lemon juice
½ onion, chopped
1 medium apple (Granny Smith), peeled and diced
⅓ cup bourbon or apple cider

Pat the pork chops dry. Rub each on both sides with cut sides of the garlic clove and sprinkle with sage. In a large skillet over medium heat, combine margarine and hot sauce and heat until mixture sizzles. Add chops and sauté 12-14 minutes, turning once, until they are golden brown on both sides and cooked through. Remove from pan to a serving dish, sprinkle with lemon juice and keep warm. Add onion to the skillet and sauté over medium heat for 1 minute. Stir in apple and sauté 1 minute longer. Add bourbon and cook, stirring for 1 minute. Spoon mixture over the pork chops and serve.

Debi Barrett-Hayes   *4 servings*

SPICY PORK ROAST

4-5 pound boneless pork roast
4 scallions, finely chopped
3 cloves garlic, finely chopped
2 jalapeno peppers, finely chopped
¼ tablespoon salt
¼ tablespoon pepper

Mix together scallions, garlic, peppers, salt and pepper. Place in center of pork roast, roll and tie securely. Rub salt on outside. Wrap in heavy foil. Cook in a 350° oven for 2 ½-3 hours, (or 30-45 minutes per pound). About 30 minutes before done, open foil and let brown.

Sandra Preston   *6 to 8 servings*

PINEAPPLE PORK ROAST

  1 loin of pork
     dash of salt
     dash of white pepper
 ½ cup brandy or sherry
 ½ cup dry wine
  8 tablespoons margarine
 ½ cup unsweetened pineapple juice
  6 slices of pineapple
  2 tablespoons sugar
  1 medium onion, finely chopped
  1 clove of garlic, finely chopped
 ½ green pepper
 ½ red pepper
  1 teaspoon tomato paste
  1 teaspoon ham glaze (Recipe in "Accompaniments")
  2 teaspoons flour
  1 cup chicken bouillon
  1 small can mandarin oranges
     sprinkle of orange rind

Preheat oven to 375°. Trim fat from pork. Score meat. Season inside and out with salt, pepper and ¼ cup of sherry. Tie roast up with a string into a bundle. Place on roasting pan and top with 3 tablespoons melted margarine and ¼ cup of pineapple juice. Roast 45-50 minutes, basting frequently with excess juices. Each time you baste, add a little more pineapple juice. Take pineapple slices and dry with paper towels, then fry in 3 tablespoons of margarine. Sprinkle with sugar and brown slightly. Make sauce by melting 2 tablespoons margarine with onion, garlic and peppers. Cook slowly over low heat 5 minutes. Do not brown vegetables. Add orange rind, tomato paste, ham glaze and flour. Add ¼ cup of sherry, dry wine and 1 cup chicken bouillon. Simmer 10 minutes and add mandarin oranges. Slice cooked pork and serve with alternating pineapple rings. Spoon sauce over pork.

Debi Barrett-Hayes   *6 servings*

HAM LOAF

2 pounds ground smoked ham
1 pound ground pork
1 cup ground bread crumbs
1 cup onion, finely chopped
1 cup tomato juice
2 eggs
1 cup melted butter
½ cup tomato sauce
1 cup brown sugar
⅔ cup vinegar
⅔ cup mustard
4 egg yolks, beaten
2 tablespoons horseradish

Mix ham, pork, bread crumbs, onion, tomato juice and eggs. Place mixture in a loaf pan and bake for 1 ¼ hours in a 350° oven. Meanwhile, in a saucepan, combine butter, tomato sauce, brown sugar, vinegar and mustard. Heat thoroughly. Add beaten eggs slowly, stirring constantly and heat until thickened. Add horseradish. Serve sauce over loaf.

Marty Blankenship   *10 servings*

Use eggs directly from the refrigerator when separating egg whites and yolks. They will break cleanly and the yolk of a cold egg is less likely to shatter than one at room temperature.

SCALLOPED POTATOES AND HAM

    2   cups ham, cubed
    6   medium potatoes, peeled and thinly sliced
    ¼   cup finely chopped onion
    ⅓   cup all-purpose flour
    2   cups milk

Layer half of the ham and then half of the potatoes in the bottom of a casserole dish. Put half of onions and flour over potatoes. Season with pepper. Repeat entire process. Cover entire mixture with milk. Cover dish and bake for 1 hour, 15 minutes in a 350° oven .

Variation: Cover cooked casserole with bread crumbs and melted margarine and bake 15 minutes uncovered, until browned.

Cheryl Garrison   *4 servings*

SAUSAGE-VEGETABLE DINNER

    2   pounds polish sausage
    5   medium baking potatoes
    1   medium green pepper, cut into strips
    1   (16 ounce) can French style green beans, drained
    1   medium cabbage, quartered
    1   medium onion, quartered
    ½   teaspoon salt
    ¼   teaspoon pepper
    1   cup water

Cut sausage diagonally into ½-inch slices. Wash and peel potatoes and cut into ⅓-inch crosswise slices. Layer sausage, potatoes and next 5 ingredients in order given, in a large Dutch Oven (1 layer of each) sprinkling each vegetable layer with salt and pepper. Add water and bring to a boil. Cover, reduce heat and simmer 45 minutes until vegetables are tender. Check to make sure water does not completely disappear, otherwise sausage will burn.

Shari Cromar   *4 to 6 servings*

MAZETTI

　¾　cup chopped celery
　¼　cup margarine
　1　cup minced onion
　¾　cup chopped green pepper
　1　pound ground chuck
　1　pound ground pork
1 ½　teaspoons salt
　½　teaspoon pepper
　12　ounces wide noodles
　¼　cup margarine
　1　(4 ounce) can mushrooms, undrained
　2　(10 ½ ounce) cans tomato soup
　　　grated cheese

Cook celery until tender in enough water to cover. Drain and reserve liquid. In a large skillet, sauté onion and green pepper in margarine for 5 minutes. Stir in ground chuck, pork, salt and pepper; cook uncovered, until meat loses its red color. Cook noodles; drain and rinse. Turn noodles into a 3 quart casserole dish, toss with ¼ cup margarine. Stir in meat mixture, celery, mushrooms and tomato soup. Mix well. Cover with cheese. Bake uncovered in a 400° oven for 1 hour, 15 minutes.

Inez B. Dasher   *6 to 8 servings*

 Consider the flavor possibilities when selecting onions. The small white onion and the large Bermuda or Spanish onion are usually mild in flavor. Globe types (red, brown, small yellow onions) are stronger flavored.

FOILED CHICKEN WITH LEMON AND HERBS

6 boneless, skinless chicken breast halves
2 tablespoons basil
2 tablespoons parsley
4 tablespoons sweet butter
  salt and freshly ground pepper to taste

Mix herbs and butter together into a paste. Generously coat the chicken breasts and place each one on a sheet of heavy-duty aluminum foil. Arrange 1-2 lemon slices over each breast and seal edges of foil tightly. Bake on a baking sheet in a 350° oven for 30 minutes. Allow each person to open their own packet, at table or tail-gate.

Hint: For fun, shape foil packets into footballs, hearts or any shape to suit your fancy. Can be made ahead of time and frozen before cooking. Thaw packets and cook on the grill for 30-40 minutes.

Shirley Unger   *6 servings*

CHICKEN BREASTS

4 chicken breast halves
  salt and pepper to taste
4 slices Swiss cheese
1 cup herb-seasoned cornbread stuffing mix
1 can cream of chicken soup
¼ cup white cooking wine
¼ cup butter or margarine

Salt and pepper chicken and place in a greased casserole dish. Place slices of Swiss cheese on top of chicken. Mix together soup and white wine; pour on top of chicken. Sprinkle stuffing mix on top. Melt butter and drizzle on top. Bake for 45 minutes in a 350° oven.

Nancy Brantly   *4 servings*

CHICKEN ITALIANO

1 ½	pounds chicken parts (approximately)
2	tablespoons shortening
1	can cheddar cheese soup
1	small fresh tomato, chopped
½	small onion, chopped
½	teaspoon garlic powder
¼	teaspoon oregano

Brown chicken in shortening, pour off fat. Sprinkle all other ingredients over chicken in the skillet. Cover with the can of soup. Simmer, covered, about 45 minutes, until tender. Uncover the last few minutes or until thickened. Stir occasionally to prevent sticking.

Note: Do not add salt.

Maxine Doster

CHICKEN PARMIGIANA

4	chicken breasts
	olive oil for frying
1	cup Italian bread crumbs
½	cup flour
1	tablespoon garlic powder or salt
1	tablespoon pepper
2	eggs, beaten
¼	cup shredded mozzarella cheese
1	(15 ounce) jar or larger spaghetti sauce

Mix together bread crumbs, flour, garlic powder and pepper. Dip chicken in egg, then roll in bread crumb mixture. Fry chicken breasts in olive oil. Place in a baking dish. Top with spaghetti sauce and mozzarella cheese. Bake in a 350° oven for 30 minutes. Serve with side dish of spaghetti.

Mary Schaber   *4 servings*

CHICKEN WITH LEMON SAUCE

- ¾ pound skinless, boneless chicken breasts
- 6 tablespoons cornstarch
- 2 tablespoons flour
- 8 cups oil for frying
- 1 sliced lemon

MARINADE
- ½ teaspoon salt
- 2 teaspoons rice wine or dry sherry
- 1 teaspoon soy sauce
- 1 egg yolk
- ⅛ teaspoon pepper

LEMON SAUCE
- ¼ cup sugar
- ¼ cup chicken broth
- 2 tablespoons water
- ½ teaspoon salt
- 2 teaspoons cornstarch
- 1 teaspoon sesame oil
  juice of 1 lemon (about ¼ cup)

Cut chicken into small pieces. Combine marinade ingredients in a medium bowl. Add chicken; mix well. Let stand 15 minutes. Combine ingredients for lemon sauce in a bowl; mix well and set aside. Mix together cornstarch and flour. Coat chicken pieces with flour mixture. Heat 8 cups of oil in a wok over medium heat to 350°. Reduce heat to low. Carefully lower chicken in hot oil. Deep fry until light golden brown. Remove chicken and drain well on paper towels. Remove all but 1 teaspoon oil from wok. Heat remaining oil in wok over medium heat. Stir lemon sauce into hot oil until sauce is glossy. Place chicken chunks on a serving platter and pour lemon sauce over chicken. Garnish with lemon slices. Serve immediately.

Marty Blankenship   *4 servings*

CHICKEN & DUMPLINGS

3 ½ pounds of chicken breast cut into small pieces
       salt and pepper
3   tablespoons margarine
2   celery stalks, chopped
1   medium onion, chopped
3   tablespoons all-purpose flour
2 ½ cups chicken stock/broth or bouillon
2   cups of cream

Heat oven to 300°. Wash chicken and lightly salt and pepper. In a large skillet melt margarine and brown the chicken over medium heat. Remove and store in oven. Add chopped celery and onions until they wilt, then add flour and cook, stirring constantly for 5 minutes. Add broth and cream and reduce the heat to low. Simmer for 30 minutes. Prepare dumplings.

DUMPLINGS

2   cups all-purpose flour
1   teaspoon baking powder
¼   teaspoon baking soda
1   teaspoon salt
3   tablespoons margarine
¾   cup milk
¼   cup dill
1 ½ quarts of chicken stock or bouillon

Sift dry ingredients into a bowl. Add melted butter and milk and blend until smooth. Fold in dill. Boil stock in a large pot. Drop spoonfuls of dumpling mix into stock. Cover and cook for 5 minutes. Poach dumplings until puffed and cooked in center.

Remove chicken from oven (having cooked approximately 45 minutes). Serve warm with freshly cooked dumplings.

Debi Barrett-Hayes

KRAUT CHICKEN

  4   boneless, skinless chicken breast halves
  1   cup Bavarian style sauerkraut
  ½   cup shredded mozzarella cheese
  1   cup honey Dijon ranch dressing
  ¼   cup Parmesan cheese

Place chicken on cookie sheet covered with aluminum foil. Place the rest of the ingredients, in order, on each piece of chicken. Bake uncovered for 30 minutes in a 350° oven.

Variation: May substitute light honey Dijon ranch dressing and low fat cheeses.

Tammy Barkve   *4 servings*

CHICKEN WITH TARRAGON CAPER SAUCE

  2   boneless chicken breast halves, split
  ½   teaspoon olive oil
  2   teaspoons capers
  ¼   teaspoon dried tarragon
  ⅓   cup whipping cream
  ½   teaspoon lemon juice
  1   tablespoon margarine

Flatten chicken and season with salt and pepper. In a medium skillet, cook chicken in oil at medium high heat for 5 minutes on each side. Remove chicken. Add cream, capers, lemon juice and tarragon, and bring almost to a boil. Remove from heat and add margarine. Pour over chicken.

Dan Hoppe   *2 servings*

CHICKEN BREAST ALFREDO

    6   boneless, skinless chicken breast halves
    ½   cup flour
    3   eggs, beaten
    3   tablespoons water
    ½   cup grated Parmesan cheese
    ½   teaspoon salt
    1   cup bread crumbs
    3   tablespoons butter or margarine
    2   tablespoons vegetable oil
    6   slices mozzarella cheese

Coat chicken with flour. Mix eggs, water, Parmesan cheese and salt. Dip pieces in egg mixture and bread crumbs. Heat butter and oil in a large skillet. Cook chicken over medium heat until brown (5 minutes). Remove to a 8x12 inch baking dish. Heat oven to 425°.

CHEESE SAUCE
    1   cup whipping cream
    ¼   cup water
    ¼   cup butter or margarine
    ½   cup grated Parmesan cheese
    ¼   cup dried parsley

Heat cream, water and butter in a 1 quart saucepan until butter melts. Add cheese, cook and stir over medium heat 5 minutes. Stir in parsley. Pour sauce over chicken. Top each piece with slice of cheese. Bake until cheese melts and chicken is tender, about 15 minutes.

Martha Eacker   *6 servings*

CHICKEN BREASTS IN PORT

  2   skinless, boneless chicken breasts
  ½   cup all-purpose flour
  1   teaspoon salt
  ¼   teaspoon nutmeg
  ¼   teaspoon fresh ground black pepper
  6   tablespoons butter
1 ½   cups heavy cream
  ¼   cup port wine
  ½   pound fresh mushrooms, sliced

Place chicken breasts between pieces of waxed paper and pound lightly with a wooden mallet or the bottom of a skillet. Combine the flour, salt, nutmeg and pepper; dredge the chicken pieces in the mixture. Melt 4 tablespoons of the butter in a heavy skillet and brown the chicken on both sides. Remove the chicken from skillet and add 1 cup of the cream, stirring constantly. Bring to a boil and simmer two minutes. Add the wine and return the chicken pieces to the skillet. Cover and simmer about 20 minutes. Meanwhile, in another skillet, melt the remaining butter and cook the mushrooms, stirring, until they are wilted. Add the remaining cream and bring to a boil. Pour this over the chicken and add salt and pepper to taste. Cover again and simmer 10 minutes longer. Serve hot.

Candy Mitchell   *4 servings*

APRICOT CHICKEN

  1   package dry onion soup mix
  1   small jar apricot preserves
  1   bottle Russian dressing (small)
  1   whole chicken, cut up

Mix first three ingredients together and pour over chicken pieces. Bake uncovered in a 350° oven for approximately 1 hour.

Tammy Brizzi   *4 to 6 servings*

CHICKEN POT PIE

1 cup chopped onion
1 cup chopped celery
1 cup chopped carrots
⅓ cup butter, melted
½ cup flour
2 cups chicken broth
1 cup half and half
1 teaspoon salt
¼ teaspoon pepper
2 cups chopped, cooked chicken
1 pie crust

Sauté onion, celery and carrots in butter for 10 minutes. Add flour, stirring well. Cool 1 minute, stirring constantly. Combine broth and half and half; gradually stir into vegetable mixture. Cook over medium heat, stirring constantly until thickened and bubbly. Stir in salt and pepper. Add chicken, stirring well. Pour into an 8x8 inch casserole dish. Top with pie crust. Cut slits in crust to allow steam to escape. Bake uncovered in a 400° oven for 40 minutes.

Martha Eacker   *4 servings*

To prevent pie crust from overbrowning, place a strip of aluminum foil over the edges. Remove during last fifteen minutes of baking.

CHICKEN DIVAN

2 (10 ounce) packages frozen broccoli
2 cups cooked chicken, diced
1 can cream of chicken soup
1 can cream of mushroom soup
1 cup mayonnaise
1 teaspoon lemon juice
½ teaspoon curry power
½ cup cheese, shredded
½ cup bread crumbs
1 tablespoon butter
3 tablespoons dry sherry

Cook broccoli in salted water until tender. Drain. Place broccoli and chicken in a 9x13 inch casserole dish. Combine mayonnaise, lemon juice, curry powder and soup. Pour over chicken. Melt butter; pour over crumbs and toss well. Spread crumbs and cheese evenly on top. Bake in a 375° oven for 20-25 minutes.

Tammy Barkve   *6 servings*

CHICKEN IN WINE SAUCE

8 boneless chicken breast halves
1 can mushroom soup
½ cup dry white wine
½ cup sour cream

Arrange chicken in a baking dish. Mix together soup and wine. Pour mixture over chicken. Bake uncovered in a 350° oven for about 45 minutes. Remove chicken from sauce. Stir sour cream into sauce. Return chicken to sauce and heat another 15 minutes in oven. Serve over rice.

Jan James/Donna Peacock   *8 servings*

BAKED TOMATOES STUFFED WITH CHICKEN & SPINACH

¼   cup chopped onion
1   cup skim milk
¼   cup flour
2   teaspoons chicken bouillon
4   slices Swiss cheese, cut into pieces
2   cups chopped, cooked chicken
1   (10 ounce) package frozen chopped spinach, thawed
       and drained
4   large tomatoes, tops cut off and insides scooped out

Preheat oven to 350°. In a medium saucepan, cook onion in ¼ cup water over medium heat until tender. In a small bowl, combine milk, flour and bouillon; stir until smooth. Add to onion. Cook and stir until mixture thickens. Add cheese and remove from heat. Stir until cheese melts; set aside. In a medium bowl, combine chicken, spinach and 1 cup of sauce. Mix well and stuff tomatoes. Place in an 8x8x2 inch baking dish, pour ½ cup water around tomatoes. Cover and bake 30 minutes, until hot. Serve with remaining sauce.

Debi Barrett-Hayes   *4 servings*

One 3 ½ pound chicken will yield approximately 3 cups diced cooked chicken.

CHICKEN WITH ARTICHOKES AND PISTACHIO NUTS

2 tablespoons margarine
1 tablespoon olive oil
1 clove of garlic, finely chopped
2 shallots, finely chopped
¼ pound mushrooms, sliced
1 (14 ounce) can quartered artichoke hearts, drained
1 ½ pounds boneless, skinless chicken breasts cut into 1 inch pieces
½ cup dry vermouth
1 teaspoon dried basil
½ pound pasta shells, cooked and drained
¼ cup shelled pistachio nuts
2 tablespoons grated Parmesan cheese

In a large frying pan, melt butter and oil over medium heat. Add garlic and shallots; cook, stirring for 1 minute, until tender. Add mushrooms and artichokes; cook about 3 minutes, until mushrooms are lightly browned. Add chicken, cook about 3 minutes, stirring constantly until chicken turns opaque. Add vermouth and basil. Bring to a boil. Reduce heat and simmer for 5 minutes. Serve over pasta. Sprinkle with pistachio nuts and Parmesan cheese.

Shallots are onions that have distinctive bulbs made up of cloves (like garlic). When cooking shallots, cook just until tender. Do not let them brown as they will become bitter.

PECAN-BREADED CHICKEN WITH MUSTARD SAUCE

8 tablespoons margarine
3 tablespoons Dijon mustard
6 ounces finely chopped pecans, about 1 ½ cups
8 skinless, boneless chicken breast halves, pounded
    to ¼-inch thickness
1 tablespoon vegetable oil
⅔ cup light sour cream
½ teaspoon salt
¼ teaspoon freshly ground pepper

In a small saucepan, melt 6 tablespoons margarine. Whisk in 2 table-spoons of mustard until blended; scrape into a shallow dish. Place pecans in another shallow dish. Dip chicken in margarine, then dredge in pecans. In a large frying pan, heat remaining margarine and oil over medium heat. Add chicken and cook 3 minutes each side until lightly browned and tender. Remove to a serving platter and cover with foil to keep warm. Discard all but 2 tablespoons fat from pan and reduce heat to low. Add sour cream. Whisk in remaining mustard, salt and pepper. Blend well. Cook just until heated through; DO NOT BOIL. Serve over chicken.

Debi Barrett-Hayes   *4 servings*

 Shelled pecans can be kept in the freezer for up to two years in an airtight bag.

OVENBAKED CHICKEN KIEV

       4 ounces Neufchatel cheese
       1 tablespoon freeze-dried chives
       8 skinless, boneless chicken breast halves
      ¾ teaspoon butter-flavored salt
      ½ teaspoon dried whole thyme
      ½ teaspoon dried whole marjoram
      ¼ teaspoon pepper
       1 egg
       1 tablespoon skim milk
      ½ cup seasoned dry bread crumbs
          vegetable cooking spray

Slice cheese into 8 equal pieces and place on waxed paper; sprinkle with chives. Cover and freeze 30 minutes or until firm. Place each chicken breast between 2 sheets of waxed paper; flatten chicken to ¼ inch thickness, using a meat mallet or rolling pin. Combine salt, thyme, marjoram and pepper; sprinkle over both sides of chicken breast. Fold long sides of chicken over cheese; tuck ends and secure with wooden toothpicks. Combine egg and skim milk in a shallow dish. Dip chicken rolls in egg mixture; roll in bread crumbs. Place chicken, seam side up, in a 2 quart baking dish coated with cooking spray. Bake in a 425° oven for 15 minutes; turn chicken rolls and bake an additional 25 minutes.

Debi Barrett-Hayes   *8 servings*

Store all spices and herbs in tightly closed containers in a cool place, away from the heat of the stove.

HUNGARIAN CHICKEN

2 ½ pounds frying chicken pieces
⅓ cup flour
2 tablespoons vegetable oil
1 medium onion, chopped
½ pound tomatoes, chopped
3 tablespoons lite soy sauce
1 tablespoon paprika
¼ teaspoon caraway seed, crushed
¼ pound fresh mushrooms, sliced
¼ cup sour cream

Coat chicken pieces with flour and brown on all sides in hot oil in large skillet over medium heat. Remove and drain on paper towels; wipe skillet clean. Add onions, tomatoes, soy sauce, paprika and caraway seeds to same skillet, stirring to combine. Bring to boil; add chicken pieces, skin side down and simmer covered, 30 minutes. Turn pieces over, add mushrooms and simmer 15 minutes longer or until chicken is tender. Remove chicken to warm serving platter. Remove skillet from heat, stir in sour cream. Heat over medium heat but do not boil. Return chicken pieces to skillet, turning pieces over to coat both sides with sauce. Serve over noodles.

Candy Mitchell   *4 servings*

 Start a collection of chicken scraps in a labeled bag in the freezer for making broth and soup. Include bones, wing tips, skin, giblets (except for livers) and other unused parts.

CHICKEN ENCHILADAS

4   chicken breasts, cooked and cut into strips
1   (16 ounce) carton sour cream
2-3 cans cream of chicken soup
1   pound Cheddar cheese, grated
2   small cans chopped green chilies
    green onions diced to taste
6-8 tortillas

Mix soup, sour cream and green chilies in a saucepan until warm. Set aside. In a mixing bowl, combine cheese, green onions and chicken. Fill each tortilla with cheese mixture and add some sauce. Roll tortilla and place in baking dish. Spoon the rest of the sauce mixture on top of tortillas. Cook, uncovered in a 350° oven for 30 minutes.

Variation: Add jalepenos for a spicy version.

Hint: For a lower fat version, substitute no fat sour cream and light Cheddar cheese.

Holly Mitchell   *8 servings*

When peeling and chopping fresh jalapeno peppers, always wear rubber gloves and keep hands away from face and eyes. Capsaicin, the compound that causes the pepper's hot flavor is also a potent skin irritation.

CHICKEN AND BLACK BEAN ENCHILADAS

3-4 pounds skinless, boneless chicken breasts
3 slices bacon
2 cloves garlic, minced
1 ½ cups picante sauce
1 (16 ounce) can black beans, undrained
1 large red bell pepper, chopped
1 teaspoon ground cumin
¼ teaspoon salt
½ cup sliced green onions
12 flour tortillas
1 ½ cups shredded Monterey Jack cheese

Cut chicken into short, thin strips. Cook bacon in 10 inch skillet until crisp. Remove to paper towel; crumble. Pour off all but 2 tablespoons of drippings. Cook and stir chicken and garlic in drippings until chicken is no longer pink. Stir in ½ cup of the picante sauce, beans, pepper, cumin and salt. Simmer until thickened, about 7-8 minutes, stirring occasionally. Stir in green onions and bacon. Spoon heaping ¼ cup of bean mixture down the center of each tortilla; top with 1 tablespoon cheese. Roll up each tortilla; place seam side down in a lightly greased 13x9 inch baking dish. Spoon remaining 1 cup picante sauce evenly over enchiladas. Bake in a 350° oven for 15 minutes, covered. Top with remaining cheese; return to oven for about 3 minutes.

Hint: Can be topped with shredded lettuce, chopped tomatoes, sour cream and avocado slices. May be frozen before adding extra toppings.

Candy Mitchell   *6 servings*

 Poultry is one of the most economical sources of high-quality protein. In fact, chicken and turkey are actually lower in calories than most other meats, serving for serving.

VEGETABLE TURKEY PIE

2 cups frozen mixed vegetables
2 tablespoons water
⅓ cup ketchup
1 teaspoon prepared mustard
1 egg, beaten
½ cup fine, dry seasoned bread crumbs
½ cup skim milk
¼ teaspoon salt
dash of pepper
1 pound ground turkey or chicken
1 package (4 servings) instant mashed potatoes
3 slices American cheese, cut into triangles

Combine vegetables and water in a micro-safe 1 quart casserole dish and cook, covered, on HIGH for 4-6 minutes or until tender-crisp. Stir mustard and ketchup together; set aside. Combine egg, bread crumbs, milk, salt, pepper and turkey, mixing well. Press into bottom and up the sides of a 9 inch micro-safe pie plate. Cover loosely with wax paper. Cook, covered, on HIGH 6-8 minutes or until done, giving dish a ½ turn once. Drain excess fat. Prepare potatoes according to package directions. Spread potatoes over turkey. Top with vegetables. Arrange cheese over vegetables. Cook, uncovered, on HIGH 1-2 minutes or until cheese melts.

Brunetta S. Pfaender   *6 servings*

 Ground turkey is a blend of white and dark turkey meats and substitutes well for ground beef in many recipes. The fat content can vary, depending on the proportion of dark meat used, as it is higher in fat.

BAKED STUFFED PEPPERS

          6 large green peppers
          1 large onion, chopped
             salt and pepper to taste
          3 eggs
          1 clove garlic, minced
          1 pound ground turkey meat
      1 ½ cups cooked rice
             garlic salt to taste
          1 (16 ounce) can tomato or spaghetti sauce
             Parmesan cheese

Cut tops off green peppers and remove seeds. Put remaining tops aside temporarily. Place peppers in a large pot and parboil. In a mixing bowl, combine ground turkey meat, chopped onion, salt, pepper, minced garlic, garlic salt, rice and eggs. Fill each pepper with this mixture and place in a baking dish. Chop pepper tops into small pieces and sprinkle on top of each stuffed pepper. Pour spaghetti sauce over the tops of all and sprinkle with Parmesan cheese. Bake in a 350° oven for 1 ½ hours.

Julie Blankenship   *6 servings*

SO GOOD LEFTOVER TURKEY

      2-3 cups cooked, boneless turkey, cut into pieces
          2 cans cream of mushroom or cream of chicken soup
          1 small can pimiento peppers
          3 celery stems, cut in pieces
             pepper
          ½ can almonds

Cook celery in broth or margarine until tender. Mix all ingredients together. Heat thoroughly. Serve on rice, toast points or fried noodles.

Nelle Sewell   *4 to 6 servings*

VENISON STEAK

    venison steak
1   inch of cooking oil
2   cups flour
    Virginia Seasoning

Remove all bones from venison steak and soak in cool water; drain well, until almost dry. Add Virginia seasoning and cover with flour. Preheat cooking oil in frying pan. Place meat in pan and cook 3-5 minutes; then turn over and cook until brown. Drain well.

VIRGINIA SEASONING
1   box of salt
1 ½   ounces black pepper
2   ounces red pepper
1   ounce garlic powder
1   ounce chili powder
1   ounce monosodium glutamate or seasoned salt
          flavor enhancer

Mix well and store in a sealed jar. Use when cooking or grilling venison, chicken, pork, fish or vegetables.

Virginia Sessions

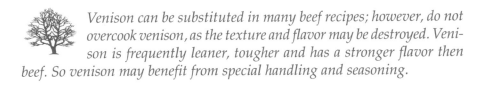

Venison can be substituted in many beef recipes; however, do not overcook venison, as the texture and flavor may be destroyed. Venison is frequently leaner, tougher and has a stronger flavor then beef. So venison may benefit from special handling and seasoning.

VENISON RAGOUT

3 pounds boned venison
1 cup vinegar
½ cup water
   seasoned salt flavor enhancer
   salt and pepper to taste
2 cups chopped celery
2 cups chopped onion
   pinch of rosemary
1 cup water
¼ cup flour
¼ cup melted butter
¼ cup red Burgundy wine
½ pint sour cream

Marinate venison overnight in vinegar, ½ cup of water, seasoned salt flavor enhancer, salt and pepper. Drain venison. Place in a casserole dish with celery, onion, rosemary and 1 cup of water. Cover and braise in a 350° oven for 2 hours. Remove the venison from the casserole dish. Slice it and keep it warm in a chafing dish. Strain stock. Combine flour and butter. Stir until smooth. Add to stock and cook, stirring constantly, until thickened. Stir in wine and sour cream. Pour over venison and serve from chafing dish.

6 to 8 servings

 Venison is tenderized by rubbing with a lemon half dipped in vinegar or by soaking in Italian salad dressing. Allow to marinate for at least an hour, up to overnight.

VENISON SCALLOPINI

  4   thin venison steaks
      salt and pepper to taste
 ½   cup finely grated Parmesan cheese
 ⅓   cup cooking oil
  1   clove garlic
  4   tablespoons lemon juice
 ⅔   cup dry red wine
 ⅔   cup beef stock or consommé
 ½   teaspoon basil
 ½   teaspoon oregano

Salt and pepper the venison steaks; sprinkle Parmesan cheese on both sides, rubbing in well. Cut the steaks into small portions. Brown crushed clove of garlic in hot cooking oil in a large skillet; remove garlic and discard. Lightly brown the strips of venison on both sides, then add remaining ingredients. Cover the skillet and simmer for about 20 minutes. Garnish with lemon slices.

4 servings

 For extra tenderness, beat venison with a mallet before marinating.

VENISON CURRY

3 tablespoons flour
2 teaspoons salt
¼ teaspoon pepper
2 pound boneless venison, cut into 1 inch cubes
3 tablespoons oil or drippings
1 bay leaf
1 teaspoon curry powder
3 whole cloves
2 teaspoons sugar
1 large onion, thinly sliced
1 clove garlic
1 cup water
3 large tart apples, cored and cut in eighths

Combine flour, salt and pepper. Dredge meat in seasoned flour and brown in oil. Pour off drippings. Add bay leaf, curry powder, cloves, sugar, onion, garlic and water. Cover tightly and cook slowly for 2 hours. Add apple wedges and continue cooking for 45 additional minutes. Discard bay leaf and garlic. Serve over cooked rice, if desired.

4 to 6 servings

 Serve venison curry with any of the following side dishes: hard-boiled eggs, finely chopped; sliced, fresh bananas; crisp chopped bacon; or a mixture of chopped onions, green peppers and cucumbers mixed with yogurt.

VENISON OR ELK STEW

      2   pounds venison or elk
          salt and pepper to taste
          flour
    4-5   cups water
      1   cup chopped celery
   1 ½   cups sliced carrots
      8   small whole yellow onions
      2   (16 ounce) cans of whole tomatoes
      1   (8 ounce) can whole kernel corn, drained
      1   (8 ounce) can butter beans or lima beans
      3   cups cubed potatoes

Cut meat (steak, roast or loin is suitable) into 1 ½ inch cubes. Salt, pepper and flour the cubes. Deep fry until brown, 4-5 minutes. Place browned meat in a large pot with water. Bring to a boil and add celery. Cook until celery is tender. Add carrots; simmer for 20 minutes. Add onions; cook 20-25 minutes. Add tomatoes, corn, beans and potatoes. Season to taste and simmer until all ingredients are tender. Serve over cooked rice.

John T. Sewell, Jr.   *10 to 12 servings*

 Trim off fat from venison before cooking or freezing, as the venison fat becomes strong.

GRILLED VENISON LOIN (BACKSTRAP)

venison loin
salt
pepper
seasoned salt
bacon

Remove all white sinew from the loin. Season with salt, pepper and seasoned salt. Wrap loin with bacon and secure with wooden toothpicks. Repeat seasoning. Cook over charcoal fire or gas grill (high heat) until bacon is done, approximately 20 minutes. Turn several times in order to cook on all sides. Slice in ¼ inch thick pieces to serve.

John T. Sewell

BAKED QUAIL

8   quail, whole or breasts
3   cups milk
    salt and pepper to taste
1   cup flour (or bread crumbs)
1   stick butter
1   chopped onion
1   chopped sweet green pepper
1   can cream of chicken soup
¼   cup white sherry wine
½   cup milk

Soak quail overnight in 3 cups of milk. Salt and pepper quail. Roll in flour. Brown in butter (do not overcook—just brown). Place in baking dish. Pour off ½ of drippings. Sauté onion and green pepper in same skillet. Add soup, wine and ½ cup of milk and mix well. Pour over quail. Cover and bake for 45 minutes in a 300° oven.

4 to 6 servings

ROAST PHEASANT WITH BRANDY AND CREAM

8 shallots, thinly sliced
¼ cup butter
3 pheasants
½ cup brandy
2 cups chicken bouillon
1 teaspoon salt
  black pepper to taste
6 slices bacon
2 cups heavy cream
¼ cup horseradish

Sauté shallots in butter in a roasting pan for 5 minutes. Add pheasants and sauté over high heat for 15 minutes or until brown on all sides. Pour some brandy into a metal ladle and the rest over the pheasants. Warm the ladle over a match, light the brandy and pour over the pheasants, flaming them. When the flames die, add bouillon, salt and pepper. Put bacon over pheasants' breasts and roast uncovered in a 375° oven for 45 minutes, basting frequently. Stir cream and horseradish into pan juices and continue roasting for 15 minutes, basting frequently.

6 servings

When sautéing, be sure that food is dry on the surface. If it is wet, it will not brown properly and steam will form which breaks the seal holding in the juices. Steam will also form if the pan is too crowded.

ROAST DUCK WITH CHAMBORD AND GRAND MARINER

2 ducks, 4 pounds each, cleaned
1 clove garlic
  salt and black pepper to taste
2 medium oranges, sliced with peel on
½ pint raspberries
3 tablespoons brown sugar
1 ½ tablespoons cornstarch
¾ cup Grand Mariner
¾ cup Chambord

Dry ducks inside and out with a clean dish cloth. Prick skin all over with a fork and leave on counter for 1 hour. Preheat oven to 350°. Pat ducks dry again and rub skin with garlic and salt. Arrange ducks on a rack in a roasting pan. Place in oven and bake for 60 minutes. Drain the fat off and return ducks to oven to bake for another 40 minutes longer. In a saucepan, combine raspberries, orange slices and brown sugar; simmer over low heat for 10 minutes. Remove orange slices and set aside. Mash raspberries and add Chambord and Grand Mariner. Whisk in cornstarch and add orange slices back to mixture. Cook over low heat until mixture thickens. Transfer ducks to a serving platter. Serve sauce over roasted ducks.

Julie Blankenship   *4 servings*

The flavor of wild fowl, such as duck or goose, is drastically affected by what the bird eats. Fish-eating fowl will often have a stronger flavor than grain- or vegetation-fed birds.

CANTONESE DUCK

        2   wild ducks, 2-2 ½ pounds each
            garlic salt
            pepper
        4   sprigs parsley
        1   lemon, halved
        6   slices bacon
        ½   cup grapefruit or lime juice
        ¼   cup dry mustard
        2   tablespoons soy sauce
        ½   cup canned apricots (or stewed ones), mashed to pulp
        1   tablespoon grated orange rind
        ¼   cup butter or margarine, melted

Sprinkle ducks inside and out with garlic salt and pepper. Place 2 sprigs of parsley and lemon half in the cavity of each duck. Cover with bacon strips and fasten with strings.

CANTONESE SAUCE: Stir grapefruit or lime juice into dry mustard. Add soy sauce, apricot pulp and grated orange rind. Heat in double boiler over hot water. If a degree of sweetness is desired, add orange marmalade, chopped candied fruits or a dash of sugar.

Preheat oven at 350°. Place ducks, breast up, in a baking pan. Bake 15 minutes per pound, or for 1-1 ½ hours. Baste frequently with melted butter or margarine and once with the Cantonese Sauce. Remove lemon and parsley from cavity and discard. Carve ducks and serve with remaining Cantonese Sauce.

4 servings

ROAST WILD DUCK

   2 wild ducks, cleaned
      salt and pepper to taste
   1 medium onion, chopped
   1 apple, cored and chopped
   1 celery stalk, chopped
   1 chopped garlic clove, chopped
   1 (10 ¾ ounce) can consommé
   1 cup dry red wine
   2 tablespoons Worcestershire sauce

Rub ducks inside and out with salt and pepper. Stuff ducks with onion, apple, celery and garlic. Place breast side down in a roasting pan. Pour consommé and red wine over ducks. Sprinkle Worcestershire sauce over ducks. Roast in a 325° oven for about 1-1 ½ hours, basting often. Turn breast side up and continue roasting for 30 minutes or until brown, basting often. Add water to maintain level of sauce, if needed.

4 servings

SMOKED WILD DUCK

   2 wild ducks, cleaned
   2 medium onions, quartered
   2 medium oranges, quartered

Stuff each duck with ½ quartered onions and oranges. Cook in smoker for approximately 1 hour on high setting. Remove stuffing before serving.

John Hamilton   *4 servings*

CORNISH HENS

   4 Cornish game hens
   1 clove garlic, quartered
   4 teaspoons tarragon
      salt and pepper
      garlic salt

CORNISH HEN BASTE
   ¾ cup margarine or butter
   ¾ cup dry white wine
   1 tablespoon tarragon

Put garlic, salt, pepper and 1 teaspoon tarragon inside each hen. Sprinkle outside of hen with garlic salt. Bake in a 450° oven for 1 hour, basting often. Serve with wild rice.

Jennifer Craig   *4 servings*

BRAISED DOVES

   4 doves
      salt and pepper to taste
      flour
   ¼ cup bacon drippings
   ½ cup milk
   1 can condensed cream of celery soup
   ½ cup chopped onion
   ¼ teaspoon caraway seeds

Sprinkle doves inside and out with salt, pepper and flour. Heat bacon fat in a skillet; add doves and brown on all sides. Add milk, soup, onion and caraway seeds. Bring to a simmer. Cover and simmer gently over low heat 20-25 minutes, or until tender, basting frequently with sauce in pan. Remove doves to serving dish. Serve sauce in side dish.

2 servings

WILD GOOSE

    1   goose (6 to 8 pounds)
        salt
        goose giblets, chopped
    2   carrots, peeled and sliced
    2   cups beef broth
    1   onion, finely chopped
   ¼   cup butter
   ¼   cup flour
   ½   teaspoon marjoram
   ½   teaspoon thyme
    1   cup sour cream
   ½   pound fresh mushrooms, sliced

Wash and salt goose. Place on rack in shallow pan. Roast, uncovered at 350° for 1 ½ hours. While goose is roasting, simmer giblets and carrots in beef broth. Sauté onion in butter. Blend in flour to make a roux, then gradually stir in giblet broth, giblets, carrots and spices. Slowly add the sour cream to gravy mixture, stirring constantly. Remove goose from pan. Pour gravy into clean roasting pan with lid. Place goose on top of gravy and sprinkle gravy with mushrooms. Place in oven, cover and bake for 2 additional hours.

Julie Blankenship   *6 servings*

 Roux is flour cooked in fat for savory sauces. Blend gently over low heat for five minutes or longer, depending upon the recipe. Be sure the roux is cooked long enough to lose the raw taste of flour; stir constantly during cooking to heat evenly.

RABBIT STEW

  6 tablespoons flour
  ½ teaspoon salt
  ¼ teaspoon pepper
  1 2 pound rabbit, skinned, cleaned and jointed
  4 slices bacon
  3 tablespoons olive oil
  1 tablespoon tomato paste
  1 clove garlic, peeled and pushed through press
1 ½ cups water
  ¾ cup red wine
12 pearl onions
12 medium mushrooms
  ¾ pound carrots, cut ½-inch slices
  ½ teaspoon dried sage
  ½ teaspoon dried thyme
  ½ teaspoon dried sweet basil
  2 bay leaves
  8 ounces tomatoes, peeled and chopped
  ½ pound shelled lima beans

Preheat oven to 325°. Mix 3 tablespoons of flour with salt and black pepper. Evenly coat rabbit joints with flour mixture. Cut bacon into 1 ½ inch slices. Sauté bacon in a skillet over moderately high heat for 6 minutes or until crisp. Remove bacon and place in a casserole dish. Drain off all but 1 tablespoon fat and add 1 ½ tablespoons olive oil to skillet. When hot, sauté ½ of rabbit pieces until golden, remove and add another 1 ½ tablespoons oil and sauté remaining rabbit. Place rabbit on top of bacon. Lower heat and blend remaining flour into juices. Cook and stir for 2 minutes. Add tomato paste and garlic and blend in water and wine. Stir until smooth. Mix in herbs, onions, mushrooms and carrots and pour over rabbit. Cover and cook for 1 hour or until rabbit is tender. Add tomatoes and beans to the pan and season with salt and pepper to taste. Cook for 20 minutes or until beans are tender. Serve with mashed potatoes.

Julie Blankenship　　　　　　　　　　　　　　　　　　*4 servings*

GINGER STEAMED BASS

1   whole Bass (4-5 pounds), cleaned
1   inch piece of fresh ginger, peeled and chopped (about ¼ cup)
1   small red chili pepper, chopped
2   ripe tomatoes, peeled and thinly sliced
1   can sliced water chestnuts
5   small carrots, peeled, thickly chopped and steamed
2   medium leeks, thickly chopped and steamed
¼   cup chopped parsley
½   cup apple cider
    non-stick vegetable spray
    salt to taste

Preheat oven to 400°. Line a large sheet of foil with parchment paper. Lightly coat paper with non-stick vegetable spray. Place fish on the parchment paper. Salt inside of Bass and stuff with vegetables and ginger. Pour cider over fish and tightly close foil over fish. Bake for 20-25 minutes.

Debi Barrett-Hayes   *4 to 6 servings*

Terms used when carving various fishes:
- *barb a lobster*
- *culpon a trout*
- *sauce a flounder*
- *splay a bream*
- *tayme a crab*
- *tusk a catfish*

CRAB IMPERIAL

½ pound crab meat, carefully picked clean
4 large eggs, beaten well
1 teaspoon dry mustard
½ cup chopped green pepper
6 tablespoons butter, melted
½ cup milk
¼ teaspoon cayenne pepper
7 teaspoons mayonnaise
1 teaspoon salt
12 saltine crackers, rolled until well crushed
    dash of Worcestershire sauce

Mix all ingredients together except crab meat. Add crab, mixing well. Turn into a lightly greased 1 ½ quart casserole dish. Place casserole dish in a pan of water. Bake in a 450° oven for 15-20 minutes.

Julie Blankenship   *4 servings*

SHRIMP NEWBURG

1 pound cooked shrimp
3 tablespoons butter
1 teaspoon lemon juice
1 teaspoon flour
½ cup half and half
2 egg yolks, slightly beaten
2 tablespoons sherry
    salt and pepper to taste

In a medium skillet, melt 2 tablespoons of butter, add the shrimp and cook for three minutes. Add lemon juice and cook one minute. Melt 1 tablespoon butter in saucepan. Stir in flour. Gradually add half and half. Stir and cook until thickened. Cool a little and add beaten egg yolks, shrimp mixture and sherry. Season to taste and add more half and half if necessary.

Beulah McGlon   *6 servings*

OYSTER BAKE

  1   quart of oysters, drained
  ¼   pound margarine
  1   medium onion, finely chopped
  ⅛   teaspoon garlic
  ⅛   teaspoon seafood seasoning
  3   large eggs, beaten well
  2   cups oyster crackers, crushed
      dash of dry mustard
      paprika
      salt and pepper to taste

Coarsely grind oysters in a food chopper/processor. Season to taste with salt and pepper. Sauté onion and garlic in margarine. Stir in oysters and seafood seasoning. Add eggs and 1 ¾ cups oyster crackers and dry mustard. Place rounded piles of mixture into individual oyster shells or ramekins. Sprinkle with remaining cracker crumbs. Place a spot of margarine on each one and sprinkle with paprika. Bake in a 350° oven for 18-20 minutes.

Debi Barrett-Hayes   *8 servings*

If baking in oyster shells, place enough rock salt in the bottom of a large shallow baking pan to support shells and keep them from tipping over.

BROILED SCALLOPS

  1   cup dry white wine
  5   tablespoons unsalted butter
  1   small onion
  3   sprigs parsley with stems
 ½   teaspoon thyme
  1   bay leaf
  2   cloves garlic, minced
  1   tablespoon fresh lemon juice
1 ½   pounds large bay or sea scallops
  1   teaspoon cornstarch mixed with 3 tablespoons cold water
  2   tablespoons grated Parmesan cheese

Bring wine, butter, onion, herbs, garlic and lemon juice to a boil. Reduce heat, add scallops and simmer until tender (about 5 minutes). Remove scallops with a slotted spoon and set aside. Boil the liquid for about 5 more minutes, reduce to simmer. The sauce will be thin. Add the cornstarch-water mixture and stir sauce until it thickens. Remove from heat and strain. Place the scallops in a baking dish. Top with sauce, sprinkle with cheese and place in broiler until browned.

Julie Blankenship   *4 servings*

 Scalloping in Apalachee Bay or St. Joe Bay is a popular summer activity. If fortunate enough to have fresh scallops, remember that only the large muscle of a scallop is eaten.

SEVICHE

        2   cups fresh shrimp (peeled and deveined) or scallops
        ½   cup coarsely chopped onion
        2   small hot peppers finely chopped, or hot sauce to taste
                (other peppers optional)
        ⅓   cup fresh lime juice
        ⅓   cup tomato juice
        ⅓   cup olive oil
        1   large tomato, peeled and chopped
    1 ½   cloves of garlic, finely minced
        ½   teaspoon chopped thyme
        1   tablespoon chopped parsley
        1   tablespoon chopped coriander
            salt and pepper to taste

Combine all ingredients and refrigerate overnight.

Note: Use only FRESH seafood in this recipe. Do not omit the lime juice. It is an essential ingredient in the recipe, as it "cooks" the seafood.

4 servings

SAUTÉED SHRIMP

        2   pounds fresh or frozen shrimp, peeled and deveined
        ½   stick butter or margarine
        1   (7 ounce) package Italian dressing mix
            lemon juice to taste (optional)

Melt butter or margarine in a saucepan. Blend in the dressing mix. Add shrimp and sauté over medium heat until done. Serve over rice or as is. This recipe is quick, easy and delicious.

Nelle Sewell   *4 servings*

SHRIMP CREOLE

1   can chicken broth
1   garlic clove
1   onion, chopped
1   cup chopped celery
1   green pepper, chopped
1   bay leaf, crushed
1   teaspoon chili powder (optional)
1   teaspoon sugar
1   teaspoon vinegar (optional)
1   (16 ounce) can tomatoes
1   can green beans or English peas
1   pound shrimp, peeled and deveined
6   slices cooked bacon
    cooked rice

Place all ingredients, except bacon and shrimp, in a large pot. Bring to a boil. Add shrimp and bacon and cook for 8-10 minutes. Do not overcook shrimp. Serve over rice.

Note: Recipe can be easily doubled or tripled.

Grace Seckel   *3 to 4 servings*

Peeling shrimp is easy either before or after cooking. Just remember that cooking shrimp in the shells adds considerable flavor.

SHRIMP ETOUFFEE

½ cup margarine
½ cup flour
1 cup chopped onions
½ cup chopped green onions
½ cup chopped green pepper
¼ cup chopped celery
2 tablespoons chopped parsley
  salt and cayenne pepper to taste
2 bay leaves
3 cups hot water
3 pounds shrimp, peeled and deveined
  cooked rice

Melt margarine in a heavy pot. Add flour. Cook until golden brown, stirring constantly. Add onions, green peppers, celery and seasonings; sauté until done (5 minutes). Add shrimp and water. Simmer uncovered approximately 45 minutes. Serve over rice.

4 to 6 servings

The black or green vein that runs along the curve of the shrimp is harmless, but is usually removed and the shrimp rinsed under running water to improve its appearance.

BRAZILIAN SHRIMP AND CHEESE CASSEROLE

    2   tablespoons butter or margarine
    1   medium onion, diced
    1   medium green pepper, diced
    1   clove of garlic, crushed
    2   fresh tomatoes, diced
    ½   teaspoon dill seed
    2   teaspoons minced parsley
    2   teaspoons minced coriander
    1   pound medium shrimp, peeled and deveined
    4   ounces cream cheese
    8   ounces shredded cheddar cheese
    8   ounces shredded mozzarella cheese
    ½   cup bread crumbs

In a medium saucepan, cook onion, garlic and green peppers in butter until softened. Add tomatoes, cook 3 minutes. Add spices and shrimp, cook over low heat until shrimp turns pink. Spread cream cheese evenly over sides and bottom of a 2 quart baking dish. Carefully pour half of shrimp mixture into casserole dish, cover with half of shredded cheeses. Add remaining shrimp mixture and cover with remaining cheeses. Top with bread crumbs. Bake in a 350° oven for 30 minutes. Serve with rice.

Cindy Mackiernan   *9 to 12 servings*

STACEY'S LOW COUNTRY BOIL

3 ½ quarts water (may need to add more to cover all ingredients later)
1 can of beer
1 tablespoon salt
½ cup white vinegar
1 bag crab boil
1 sliced lemon (optional)
12 red potatoes (cut large ones in half)
4 large onions, cut into quarters (Vidalia onions preferred)
6 ears corn on the cob, cut in halves
1 pound smoked sausage (pork preferred, but may use beef sausage if desired)
3 pounds unpeeled shrimp (remove heads)

In a six quart or larger pot, add water, beer, salt, vinegar, crab boil, potatoes, onions and lemon slices. Bring to a boil and add sausage. Cook for 25 minutes. Add corn on the cob then cook 10 more minutes at a boil. Add shrimp (unpeeled) and bring back to a boil. Serve immediately with rice.

Florence Griner   *8 to 10 servings*

Buy fresh shrimp that are firm and light-colored, with no strong odors. Refrigerate as soon as possible, making sure they are not out of the refrigerator for more than two hours. Cook within two days; or, remove heads, wash, and freeze in sealed bags.

HUNTER'S BLUEFISH WITH HORSERADISH SAUCE

1	cup sour cream
½	cup horseradish
2	tablespoons lemon juice
1	teaspoon capers
1 ½	pounds bluefish fillets
⅛	teaspoon salt
⅛	teaspoon pepper
3	tablespoons butter
	lemon slices
	parsley
	chives

Combine sour cream, horseradish, lemon juice and capers. Sprinkle fish with salt and pepper. Melt butter in a 13x9x2 inch baking dish. Remove from heat, turn fish over in the butter, coating both sides. Pour sour cream mixture over fish and bake uncovered in a 350° oven for 25 minutes or until fish flakes. Garnish with parsley, chives and lemon slices.

Note: If you double the recipe, don't double the horseradish.

Jennifer Craig   *4 servings*

 If using frozen fillets, thaw fish in milk. The milk draws out the frozen taste and provides a fresh-caught taste.

GROUPER FILLETS

4   grouper or hogfish fillets (about 4-6 ounces each)
1   medium onion, sliced paper-thin
1   clove garlic, minced
1   cup sour cream, regular or low-fat
    ground black pepper to taste

Preheat oven to 400°. Cut 4 pieces of aluminum foil large enough to wrap fillets and seal tightly. Place a fillet in center of each piece of foil. Spread sour cream over surface of fillets. Sprinkle garlic and pepper over surface. Place onion slices evenly over fillets. Seal each foil bag tightly so that no juices or steam escapes while cooking. Place sealed bags on baking sheet and bake for 10-15 minutes, depending on thickness of fillets.

Margaret Rodrigue   *4 servings*

BAKED FLOUNDER

1   flounder fillet (about 4-6 ounces)
2   slices tomato
1   slice green pepper
1   slice red pepper
1   thin slice onion
2   tablespoons melted butter
⅛   teaspoon garlic powder
    seasoned bread crumbs

Grease an 8x8 inch baking dish with 1 tablespoon of melted butter. Place tomato slices on bottom, then peppers and onion. Place fillet over the vegetables. Pour remaining melted butter over fish and top with garlic powder and a generous sprinkling of bread crumbs. Bake in a 400° oven for about 15 minutes. Place under broiler to brown bread crumbs.

Shari Cromar   *1 serving*

FLOUNDER AMBASSADOR

    4   flounder fillets (about 1 pound)
    ⅛   teaspoon salt
    ⅛   teaspoon pepper
    ½   cup chopped fresh parsley
    2   tablespoons margarine
    2   tablespoons lemon juice
    ¼   pound fresh mushrooms, sliced
    1   tablespoon all-purpose flour
    ½   cup whipping cream
    ¼   cup milk
    1   tablespoon Dijon mustard
    2   tablespoons Parmesan cheese
    1   tablespoon fine dry bread crumbs
    ¼   teaspoon paprika

Arrange fillets in a lightly greased 12x8x2 inch baking dish. Sprinkle with salt, pepper and parsley. Set aside. Combine margarine and lemon juice in a skillet. Add mushrooms and sauté 2-3 minutes. Add flour, stirring until smooth. Gradually add whipping cream and milk. Cook over medium heat, stirring constantly until mixture is thickened and bubbly. Stir in mustard and spread sauce over fillets. Sprinkle with cheese, bread crumbs and paprika. Bake in a 350° oven for 25-30 minutes or until fish is flaky.

Debi Barrett-Hayes   *4 servings*

SALMON LOAF WITH CUCUMBER SAUCE

    1   (16 ounce) can salmon, drained and flaked
    ¾   cup fine dry bread crumbs
    ⅔   cup skim evaporated milk
    ¼   cup sliced onion
    ¼   cup diced green pepper
    1   egg, beaten
    1   tablespoon lemon juice
    ¼   teaspoon celery salt
    ¼   teaspoon pepper
        vegetable spray

Combine salmon, bread crumbs, milk, onion, green pepper, egg, lemon juice, celery salt and pepper; mix well. Press mixture into 8x5x3 inch loaf pan coated with cooking spray. Bake in a 375° oven for 45-50 minutes or until done. Remove from oven and let stand 3 minutes. Remove from pan. Serve with Cucumber Dill Sauce.

6 servings

CUCUMBER DILL SAUCE
    3/4   cup plain, low-fat yogurt
    ½   cup unpeeled diced cucumber
    ¼   cup reduced-calorie mayonnaise
    1   tablespoon minced onion
    1   teaspoon chopped fresh parsley
    ¼   teaspoon dried whole dill weed
    ⅛   teaspoon salt

Combine all ingredients and mix well. Cover sauce and chill 30 minutes. Stir before serving.

1 ½ cups

OVERNIGHT SALMON STRATA

  1 (14 ¾ ounce) can salmon
  8 slices white or honey wheat bread
  1 cup frozen peas, thawed and drained
  ¼ cup chopped green pepper
  ¼ cup chopped onion
  ½ cup chopped celery
  1 tablespoon diced pimiento, rinsed and thoroughly drained
     (optional)
1 ½ cups shredded sharp cheddar cheese, divided
     milk
  4 eggs, slightly beaten
  ½ teaspoon salt
  ¼ teaspoon hot pepper sauce
  ¼ teaspoon crushed dill weed

Drain and chunk salmon; reserve liquid. Trim crusts from 5 slices of bread. Cut in half diagonally and set aside. Use remaining bread and trimmings to line the bottom of a 11x7x2 inch baking dish. Combine peas, green pepper, onion, celery and pimiento. Sprinkle over bread in baking dish. Top with ½ cup cheese, salmon, then another ½ cup cheese. Arrange bread triangles over all. Add milk to reserved salmon liquid to equal 2 cups; combine with eggs, salt, hot pepper sauce and dill weed. Pour milk mixture over bread. Cover and refrigerate at least 1 hour or overnight. Uncover and bake in a 325° oven for 1 hour or until knife inserted near center comes out clean. Sprinkle with remaining ½ cup cheese and bake 5 minutes longer. Let stand 5-10 minutes before serving.

Shari Cromar   *8 servings*

FLORIDA SNAPPER WITH GREEN PEPPERCORN SAUCE

4 (6 ounce) snapper fillets
1 tablespoon safflower or corn oil
3 tablespoons pared and diced shallots
1 tablespoon green peppercorn
1 tablespoon minced parsley
2 teaspoons arrowroot or cornstarch
1 cup chicken or vegetable broth
½ cup dry white wine

Rinse and skin snapper. Heat oil in small non-stick pan until almost smoking. Add shallots and peppercorns. Cook 1 minute, add wine and parsley. Dissolve cornstarch in broth, add to pan. Cook over medium heat for 3-4 minutes until thick. Place fillets in a greased casserole dish. Spoon sauce evenly over fillets. Cook in a 375° oven for 10-12 minutes.

Debi Barrett-Hayes   *4 servings*

Soak fresh salt-water fish in vinegar to eliminate some of the salty taste, then rinse fish under cold water.

BAKED RED SNAPPER

4   teaspoons olive oil
½   cup chopped onion
2   cloves garlic, minced
1   cup fresh mushrooms, sliced
½   cup white wine
2   medium tomatoes, peeled and chopped
½   teaspoon dried basil
¼   teaspoon dried oregano
½   teaspoon salt
½   teaspoon pepper
4   red snapper fillets (4-6 ounces each)
4   tablespoons grated Parmesan cheese
2   tablespoons fresh parsley, chopped

Preheat oven to 400°. Sauté onion and garlic in oil until onion is translucent (about 1 minute). Add mushrooms and cook until tender (about 2 minutes). Add wine and bring to boil. Add tomato and seasonings and cook, stirring occasionally until sauce thickens (about 2 minutes). In a shallow casserole dish, arrange fillets and top with sauce. Sprinkle with cheese and bake until fish flakes (15-20 minutes). Garnish with chopped parsley.

Julie Blankenship   *4 servings*

Beware of overcooking. Fish dries out quickly when exposed to heat, and will lose a lot of flavor and texture if overcooked.

MARINATED TUNA STEAKS

    2 (1 ½ pound) tuna steaks (fresh)
    ½ cup Italian dressing
    2 tablespoons chopped parsley
    1 teaspoon Worcestershire sauce
    ½ teaspoon coarse pepper
    1 lime

In cold water, soak tuna steaks in a large shallow dish with ½ of a lime squeezed on top. Soak at least 1 hour. Place tuna on foil and cover with Italian dressing, parsley, Worcestershire sauce and pepper. Marinate up to 1 day. Preheat broiler or grill. Broil or grill until flaky. Serve with remaining lime, thinly sliced.

4 servings

CHILI RELLENO CASSEROLE

    2 (7 ounce) cans green roasted chilies
    1 pound Monterey Jack cheese, grated
    1 pound cheddar cheese, grated
    4 eggs, well beaten
    3 tablespoons flour
    1 cup evaporated milk
    ½ teaspoon salt
    ¼ teaspoon pepper

Grease a 2 quart casserole dish. Alternate in layers the chilies, cheddar cheese and Monterey Jack cheese. Add flour, milk, salt and pepper to the eggs. Pour the egg mixture over chilies and cheese. Cover and refrigerate for 24 hours. Remove from refrigerator and let stand for 15 minutes. Bake in a 350° oven for 45 minutes.

Julie Blankenship   *4 servings*

BLACK BEAN BURRITOS

 1 tablespoon vegetable oil
 1 cup chopped red pepper
 6 green onions, chopped
 4 cloves of garlic, minced
 1 (15 ounce) can black beans, drained and partially mashed
⅔ cup salsa picante
 1 tablespoon cilantro, finely chopped
 2 teaspoon ground cumin
 8 hard cooked eggs, chopped
 8 (8 inch) flour tortillas
 2 cups lettuce, shredded
    low-fat sour cream and/or salsa

In a medium saucepan, stir together oil, peppers, onions and garlic. Cover and cook over medium heat, stirring occasionally, until vegetables are tender (8-10 minutes). Stir in beans, salsa, cilantro, cumin and eggs. Place spoonful of mixture on flour tortilla, top with lettuce. Add sour cream and/or salsa to taste. Roll tortilla and serve.

Debi Barrett-Hayes   *8 servings*

Green chilies are actually a whole family of hot peppers in various shapes (pear, round, long and pencil-thin). As a rule, the sharper the point, the hotter the chili.

ITALIAN SPAGHETTI AND PECAN BALLS

1 cup pecans, finely chopped
1 cup Italian seasoned bread crumbs
1 medium onion, finely chopped
2 cups colby cheese, grated (or cottage cheese)
4 egg whites
2 tablespoons olive oil
1 (16 ounce) jar meatless spaghetti sauce
8 ounces uncooked spaghetti noodles

Mix first five ingredients. Add a little water if too dry. Form into "pecan balls." Fry in oil until golden brown. Pour spaghetti sauce over "pecan balls" and heat. Cook noodles according to package directions; drain. Serve sauce and "pecan balls" over noodles.

Variation:
RICE AND GRAVY WITH PECAN BALLS: Instead of spaghetti sauce and noodles, use a can of brown gravy and serve over rice.

Nona Yaw

 Olive oils are like wines in the way their flavors are affected by the soils in which they are grown. It will become semi-solid if refrigerated; it will liquefy if allowed to warm to room temperature before using.

GARDENER'S PIZZA

1 ¾ cups flour
¼ cup enriched cornmeal
1 teaspoon baking powder
1 teaspoon salt (optional)
⅔ cup milk
¼ cup olive oil
1 (8 ounce) can pizza sauce
1 medium green pepper, cut into thin rings
1 medium onion, thinly sliced, separated into rings
1 medium zucchini, thinly sliced
2 cups mozzarella cheese, grated
¼ cup grated Parmesan cheese

Grease a 14 inch round pizza pan or 15x10 inch jelly roll pan. Combine dry ingredients. Add milk and oil; stir until mixture forms a ball. Turn out onto prepared pan; let stand 2-3 minutes. Press dough into pan; shape edge to form rim. Bake in a 425° oven about 13 minutes or until edges are very light golden brown. Spread pizza sauce over partially baked crust. Top with vegetables and cheeses. Continue baking 15-20 minutes or until cheese is melted and edges are golden brown.

Hint: For an even quicker dish, use canned pizza crust instead of making dough.

Nona Yaw   *6 servings*

FRIED TOFU

⅔ cup light soy sauce
¼ cup chopped green onions
2 small chilies, chopped
¼ cup fresh lemon juice
1 teaspoon sugar
3 cakes tofu, pressed and dry
¼ cup peanut oil
3 cups rice, cooked
1 cup roasted peanuts, chopped (or pine nuts)
2 cups bean sprouts

Make sauce by mixing soy sauce, onions, chilies, lemon juice and sugar. Blanch sprouts by washing in hot water in a colander for 1 minute. Cool and drain. Chop tofu in cubes and pat dry again with paper towels. Heat oil in a wok or frying pan. Fry tofu in hot oil until golden brown. Drain on paper towels. Place rice on individual plates, top with tofu, then sauce. Sprinkle with peanuts.

Debi Barrett-Hayes   *4 servings*

 Tofu, or bean curd, is a bland cream-colored soybean cake that absorbs the flavors of other ingredients. It is often used as a meat substitute as it is high in protein and very low in fat.

ZUCCHINI PIE

4 cups thinly sliced, unpeeled zucchini
1 cup chopped onions
½ cup butter
½ cup chopped fresh parsley
½ teaspoon salt
½ teaspoon pepper
¼ teaspoon garlic powder
¼ teaspoon dried basil
2 eggs, well beaten
1 cup grated Muenster cheese
1 cup grated mozzarella cheese
1 (8 ounce) can refrigerated crescent dinner rolls
1 teaspoon Dijon mustard

In a 10 inch skillet, cook zucchini and onion in butter until tender, about 10 minutes. Stir in seasonings. In a large bowl, blend eggs and cheese. Add vegetable mixture and mix well. Separate dough into 8 triangles and place in an ungreased 11 inch quiche pan or 10 inch pie pan; press over bottom and up sides to form crust. Spread crust with mustard. Pour vegetable mixture evenly over crust. Bake for 25 minutes or until knife inserted in center comes out clean. If crust becomes too brown, cover edges with foil. Let stand a minimum of 10 minutes before serving.

Julie Blankenship   *6 servings*

Pasta
&
Rice

Brokaw-McDougall House

Perez Brokaw arrived in Tallahassee from New Jersey in 1840. He prospered in the livery stable business, married, and began constructing his house in 1856. After his death in 1875, his daughter Phebe married a Scottish immigrant, Alexander McDougall. Thus, the name Brokaw-McDougall.

The interior and exterior of the two-story house exhibits an elegant and distinguished aura due to its mid-nineteenth century Classical Revival style architecture. Six Corinthian columns support the roof of a one-story porch which runs across the front of the house. The house is crowned by a cupola. High ceilings and large halls running the length of both floors dominate the interior of the house. Landscaping of the formal gardens surrounding the house began in 1850 with the planting of four live oak trees. The garden also contains some of Tallahassee's oldest camellias. The property was sold to the State of Florida in 1973.

BROCCOLI CHEESE STUFFED SHELLS

     1   (6 ounce) package jumbo macaroni shells (24)
     1   bunch (2 cups) broccoli, trimmed, chopped and cooked
     1   cup celery, finely chopped
     1   cup part-skim ricotta cheese
  1 ½   cups Swiss cheese, grated
     1   tablespoon onion, minced
     1   teaspoon Italian seasoning
     4   cups canned stewed tomatoes

Cook shells according to package directions; drain. In a large bowl, combine broccoli, celery, ricotta cheese, Swiss cheese, onion and Italian seasoning. Stir until well blended. Pour 1 cup of tomatoes over bottom of a 13x9x2 inch baking pan, breaking up the tomatoes with a fork. Spoon 1-2 rounded teaspoons of broccoli-cheese mixture into each shell and place open-side up in pan. Pour remaining tomatoes over and around shells. Cover pan with foil and bake in a 375° oven for 25 minutes or until heated through.

Kim Cooper   *6 servings*

Pasta is rich in carbohydrates and protein, low in sodium and cholesterol (until toppings are added). Whole wheat pasta is more nutritious and flavorful than egg pasta.

TORTELLINI WITH DILL PESTO

1 cup packed fresh parsley (preferably Italian)
⅔ cup packed fresh dill sprigs
¼ cup (2 ounces) dry-roasted peanuts
1 clove garlic
¾ cup olive oil
3 tablespoons red wine vinegar
¼ teaspoon salt
¼ teaspoon freshly ground pepper
1 (12 ounce) package frozen cheese tortellini

Puree parsley, dill, peanuts and garlic in a food processor until paste forms. With machine running, pour oil and vinegar through feed tube. Mix in salt and pepper. Cook tortellini in a large pot of boiling salted water until al dente. Drain well and return to the hot pot. Pour the pesto sauce over the tortellini and toss gently to coat. Place tortellini in shallow bowl or platter. Serve at room temperature.

Carol Sullivan

Macaroni	*1 cup uncooked = 2 ½ cups cooked*	
Noodles	*1 cup uncooked = 1 cup cooked*	
Spaghetti	*8 ounces uncooked = 4 cups cooked*	

STUFFED SHELLS FLORENTINE

1 (29 ounce) jar marinara sauce
1 (10 ounce) package chopped spinach
2 pounds ricotta cheese
1 (12 ounce) package mozzarella cheese, grated
2 eggs
2 tablespoons grated Parmesan cheese
1 (12 ounce) package jumbo pasta shells

Cook shells according to package directions. Spoon 1 cup of sauce into the bottom of a large roasting pan or ½ cup into each of two 2 quart baking dishes. Cook spinach as directed on package; drain. In a large bowl, mix together spinach, ricotta cheese, mozzarella cheese, eggs and Parmesan cheese. Using a teaspoon, fill each shell with cheese mixture. Arrange shells open side up, in single layer in roasting pan. Top with remaining sauce. Bake in a 350° oven for 15-20 minutes.

Variation:
STUFFED SHELLS WITH SAUSAGE: Substitute 1 pound bulk (hot or mild) Italian sausage, cooked, for the spinach.

Nona Yaw   *6 servings*

Pasta that is tubular (such as manicotti) or has a cup-like space (such as shells) is designed to trap sauces. These types should be used when it is desired to eat a lot of the sauce or when the sauce has chopped meat or vegetables in it.

MANICOTTI CHEESE BAKE

½   pound ground beef
½   cup onion, minced
¼   cup green pepper, chopped
⅔   cup tomato paste
1 ½ teaspoons salt
½   teaspoon pepper
1   teaspoon sugar
1 ½ teaspoons Italian seasoning
7   manicotti shells
2   cups ricotta cheese
1   cup shredded mozzarella cheese

Saute meat, onion and green pepper. Drain fat. Add paste, water, salt, pepper, sugar and Italian seasoning. Simmer 15 minutes. Boil manicotti in salted water for 4 minutes. Drain. Fill shells with combined cheeses. Place in baking dish and cover with sauce. Bake at 350° for 20-30 minutes.

Jennifer Craig   *4 servings*

 If pastas must be cooked well in advance of preparing the rest of the recipe, moisten them with butter, milk, bouillon, or tomato juice to keep them from drying out.

SPICY LENTIL SPAGHETTI

- ¾ cup onions, chopped
- 2 cloves garlic, minced
- 4 cups water
- 1 ½ cups dried lentils
- 1 teaspoon crushed red pepper
- ½ teaspoon salt
- ½ teaspoon pepper
- 1 (14 ½ ounce) can stewed tomatoes, undrained and chopped
- 1 (6 ounce) can tomato paste
- 1 tablespoon vinegar
- 1 teaspoon beef bouillon granules
- ½ teaspoon dried basil
- ½ teaspoon dried oregano
- 1 (8 ounce) package uncooked spaghetti
  cooking spray

Coat a Dutch oven with cooking spray. Add onion and garlic and sauté on medium heat for 5 minutes or until tender. Add water, lentils, red pepper, salt and pepper; stir well. Bring to a boil, cover, reduce heat and simmer for 30 minutes, stirring occasionally. Add tomatoes, tomato paste, vinegar, bouillon, basil and oregano, stirring well to combine. Bring to a boil; reduce heat and simmer, uncovered, for 45 minutes, stirring frequently. Prepare spaghetti according to package directions. Serve sauce over spaghetti.

Dianne Skinner   *6 servings*

 Lentils have been shown to help reduce cholesterol. They are inexpensive and give top nutritional value for the dollar.

MEXI-BEAN PASTA

    1   tablespoon olive oil
1 ½   cups onions, chopped
    1   clove garlic, minced
    1   (14 ½ ounce) can stewed tomatoes
    1   (14 ½ ounce) can Mexican style stewed tomatoes
    1   teaspoon chili powder
    ½   teaspoon sugar
    ¼   teaspoon oregano
    1   (15 ounce) can pinto beans, drained and rinsed
    1   (8 ounce) package pasta of your choice

In a large skillet, sauté garlic and onion in oil until tender. Stir in all remaining ingredients except beans and pasta, chopping tomatoes with stirring spoon. Bring to a boil. Cover and reduce heat; simmer for 15 minutes, stirring occasionally. Mash beans slightly. Add to tomato mixture, stirring well. Cook for 5 minutes or until thoroughly heated, stirring frequently. Meanwhile, cook pasta according to package directions. Serve sauce over pasta.

Dianne Skinner   *4 servings*

 Rich sauces should be served with a flat pasta or a shape that does not trap too much of the sauce.

PASTA WITH PEAS, TOMATOES AND FETA CHEESE

    3   tablespoons olive oil
    2   cloves garlic, minced
    1   pound rotini pasta
    2   cups frozen peas
    2   pounds (2 ½ cups) plum tomatoes, cored, peeled, seeded
        and chopped (or 1 carton cherry tomatoes, quartered)
   ½   teaspoon salt
   ¼   teaspoon pepper
   ¼   cup lemon juice
   ½   cup chopped fresh flat-leaf parsley
    6   ounces feta cheese, crumbled and drained if necessary

Heat oil in a small skillet over low heat. Add garlic; sauté 30 seconds or until just golden brown. Set aside. Cook pasta according to package directions. Two minutes before the end of the pasta cooking time, add peas to the water and continue cooking. Drain pasta and peas in a colander, then return to pot. Stir in the garlic-oil mixture, tomatoes, salt, pepper, lemon juice and parsley. Divide among six serving plates. Top with feta cheese.

Nona Yaw   *6 servings*

Feta cheese is a semi-soft, ripened Greek cheese, salty and sharp in flavor. Look for flaky white cheese. Drain before using if packed in brine.

VEGETABLE LASAGNA

3 cups sliced zucchini
3 cups mushrooms, sliced (or 8 ounces canned mushrooms)
1 cup chopped onion
3 cloves garlic, minced
1 tablespoon olive oil
1 (26 ounce) jar spaghetti sauce
1 teaspoon oregano leaves
1 (16 ounce) carton cottage cheese
1 cup grated Parmesan cheese
1 pound uncooked lasagna noodles
2 cups grated mozzarella cheese
2 tablespoons parsley flakes

Cook zucchini, mushrooms, onion and garlic in oil until tender. Stir in spaghetti sauce and oregano and simmer 15 minutes. Combine cottage cheese and Parmesan cheese. In a 13x9 inch baking dish, layer ½ each of the noodles, sauce, cottage cheese and mozzarella cheese. Repeat layers; top with parsley. Bake covered in a 350° oven for 45 minutes. Bake uncovered for 15 more minutes. Let stand 15 minutes before serving.

Variations: Substitute 3 cups cooked broccoli or spinach in place of the zucchini. Or replace ½ of zucchini with grated carrots.

Nona Yaw   *8 to 10 servings*

SOPA SECA DE FIDEO

8 ounces vermicelli, broken
3 tablespoons olive oil
½ medium onion, chopped
1 clove garlic, minced
1 tablespoon chopped bell pepper
1 tomato, peeled and chopped
2 cups chicken stock, boiling
  fresh Parmesan cheese
  sour cream

Brown vermicelli in hot oil, stirring constantly. Drain oil; push vermicelli to one side of skillet. Add onion, bell pepper and garlic; sauté until soft. Add tomato and boiling stock; cover and cook on low until liquid is absorbed, about 20 minutes (it should be dry, like rice). Top with parmesan and/or sour cream.

Shirley Donelan   *4 to 6 servings*

SUN-DRIED TOMATO SPAGHETTI SAUCE

2 cups tomatoes, diced
2 tablespoons sun dried tomatoes in olive oil, drained and
    minced
2 tablespoons fresh basil
2 tablespoons chopped fresh parsley
2 tablespoons olive oil
1 clove garlic, crushed
⅛ teaspoon freshly ground pepper
3 finely chopped anchovies or 1 teaspoon anchovy paste
2 tablespoons chopped black olives

Combine all ingredients. Stir to blend. Heat in a small heavy pan. Toss sauce with hot pasta. Serve at once.

Dan Hoppe

SPAGHETTI REINA

2 bunches fresh broccoli (or 4 (10 ounce) packages frozen broccoli spears)
4 tablespoons butter
2 cloves garlic, chopped
½ large onion, chopped
1 (16 ounce) package spaghetti
1 teaspoon basil
1 ½ cups Parmesan cheese

Cut up broccoli in bite size pieces, cover with water in a 10 quart pot and parboil. Remove broccoli, reserving all the water in the pot. Boil the pasta in ⅔ of the reserved water according to package directions. Drain pasta. In a 10x10x2 inch dish, layer spaghetti then broccoli, repeating until dish is full. Bake in a 325° oven for 20 minutes. Meanwhile, in a skillet, sauté garlic and onion in butter until soft. In the 10 quart pot, combine the remaining ⅓ reserved water, onion mixture, Parmesan cheese and basil; simmer. Serve sauce over 3x3 inch squares of the broccoli/spaghetti bake.

Mimi Reina

SASSY SPAGHETTI

1 (11 ounce) jar medium salsa
1 cup fresh mushrooms, sliced
1 tablespoon margarine
1 (15 ounce) can black beans, drained
1 (8 ounce) package spaghetti
1 cup grated Monterey Jack cheese

Sauté mushrooms in margarine in a medium saucepan. Add salsa and black beans. Let simmer, covered, to blend flavors. While sauce is simmering, cook spaghetti. Serve sauce with spaghetti and sprinkle with cheese.

Brunetta Pfaender   *4 servings*

GRILLED TOMATO SAUCE

     1 yellow onion, peeled and diced
     8 Roma tomatoes, cored and sliced
     8 large yellow tomatoes, cored and sliced
     3 cloves of garlic, minced
     2 tablespoons fresh basil, chopped
  2 ½ tablespoons fresh marjoram, chopped
     1 tablespoon fresh thyme, chopped
   2-3 cups red wine
     2 tablespoons balsamic vinegar
     1 tablespoon cracked red pepper
        salt to taste
    ¼ cup olive oil

Before starting the sauce, brush both types of tomatoes with olive oil
and grill on a very hot grill. Remove and chop. In a large sauce pot
add olive oil and heat. Start with onions and cook them until tender.
Add both tomatoes, garlic and all the herbs. Let simmer on low heat
for 3 minutes stirring often. Add red wine, vinegar and pepper and
continue to simmer for 20 minutes. Season with salt and serve over
hot pasta.

*If cooked pasta has to sit for a few minutes after draining, toss
with a tablespoon of olive or vegetable oil to keep it from clump-
ing.*

CAJUN CHICKEN PASTA

5 tablespoons butter
2 boneless, skinless chicken breast halves, cut into chunks
1 green pepper, chopped
2 teaspoons shallots, chopped
1 ¼ teaspoons Cajun spice
8 ounces heavy cream
salt and pepper to taste
linguine or fettucini

Sauté green pepper in butter 2-3 minutes. Add chicken and shallots. Continue cooking 5 minutes, stirring occasionally. Add Cajun spice, cream, salt and pepper. Continue heating over low heat. Cook pasta according to package directions. Serve sauce over pasta.

Dan Hoppe   *2 servings*

CHICKEN WITH TORTELLINI

4 chicken breasts
1 (16 ounce) package frozen cheese tortellini
1 medium onion, sliced
1 can artichoke hearts, drained and quartered
⅓ cup red wine vinegar
½ cup olive oil
2 tablespoons sugar
½ cup fresh basil, chopped

Cook the chicken breasts and cut into bite-sized pieces. Cook the tortellini according to package directions. Mix together onion and artichoke hearts in a medium bowl. Stir in remaining ingredients, then add chicken mixture and tortellini. Can be served warm or chilled.

Diana Johnson   *4 to 6 servings*

CROCK POT CHICKEN AND SPAGHETTI

- 2-3 cups chicken, cut into chunks
- 1 cup chicken broth
- 1 can cream of mushroom soup
- 1 onion, diced
- ¼ cup white wine
- 8 ounces mushrooms, sliced

Cook ingredients in a crock pot for 8-10 hours. Serve over spaghetti. Top with Parmesan cheese, if desired.

Jacqueline Singletary   *4 servings*

CHICKEN AND NOODLES

- 1 (2-3 pound) chicken
- 1 small onion, diced
- 2 carrots, sliced
- 3 stocks of celery, sliced
- 1 tablespoon parsley
- 1 tablespoon seasoned salt flavor enhancer
  salt and pepper
- 1 package wide egg noodles

Place chicken and next five ingredients in a large pot. Add water to cover chicken. Bring to a boil, lower heat and cook for one hour. Remove chicken and cook noodles in this reserved liquid. (Add salt if needed.)

Hint: Leftovers make great chicken noodle soup.

Jennifer Craig   *4 to 6 servings*

TURKEY LASAGNA

½ cup chopped onion
8 ounces fresh mushrooms, sliced
3 cloves garlic, minced
1 pound freshly ground turkey, skin removed before grinding
3 cups no-salt added tomato sauce
2 teaspoons basil
½ teaspoon oregano
fresh ground black pepper
1 (10 ounce) package frozen no-salt added chopped spinach, defrosted and squeezed dry
2 cups (1 pound) low fat cottage cheese
dash nutmeg
1 (8 ounce) package lasagna noodles
8 ounces part-skim mozzarella cheese, grated

Preheat oven to 375°. Lightly spray a 9x13 inch baking dish with vegetable oil. In a non stick skillet over medium high heat, combine onion, mushrooms, garlic and ground turkey. Sauté until turkey is no longer pink. Cover pan and continue to cook until mushrooms have released juices, then uncover and evaporate juices over high heat. Add tomato sauce, basil, oregano and pepper. Set aside. In a bowl, mix together spinach, cottage cheese and nutmeg. Set aside. Cook noodles according to package directions, omitting salt. Lay ⅓ of noodles on bottom of dish; add ½ of spinach mixture, ⅓ sauce and ⅓ of mozzarella cheese. Repeat layers once; finish with one layer noodles, ⅓ sauce and remaining cheese. Cover with aluminum foil and bake 35-40 minutes.

Mary J. Marchant   *9 servings*

For a delightful use of the left-over holiday turkey, make two casseroles. Enjoy one now, and freeze the other for a quick and easy meal for another day.

TURKEY TETRAZZINI

2   cups chopped turkey meat, cooked and drained
½   stick butter
½   onion, sliced
¼   cup flour
1   teaspoon salt
¼   teaspoon pepper
½   teaspoon poultry seasoning
⅛   teaspoon dry mustard
2   cups milk
½   cup shredded Cheddar cheese
2   tablespoons pimiento
1   (4 ounce) can mushrooms, undrained
7   ounces spaghetti, cooked and drained
⅓   cup shredded Cheddar cheese
6   green pepper strips

Melt butter. Sauté onions in butter. Blend in flour, salt, pepper, seasoning and dry mustard. Remove from heat. Gradually add milk. Stirring constantly, cook until thickens. Add ½ cup cheese and pimiento, stirring until cheese melts. Add mushrooms with liquid to white sauce. Place layer of spaghetti in a 2 quart casserole dish. Cover with turkey and sauce. Repeat and finish with layer of spaghetti. Sprinkle ⅓ cup Cheddar cheese over top. Cover and bake in a 400° oven for 20 minutes. Garnish with green pepper strips.

Jan James/Donna Peacock   *4 to 6 servings*

Select green peppers that are firm, shiny and thick-fleshed. The color should be medium to dark green.

SHRIMP AND SCALLOPS PASTA

    4   tablespoons olive oil
   12   ounces medium shrimp, peeled and deveined
   ½   teaspoon oregano
    1   teaspoon sweet basil
   ½   teaspoon pepper
    3   cloves garlic, minced
   12   ounces large bay scallops
   12   ounces chicken stock
   ½   teaspoon flour
   ½   package frozen artichokes, defrosted
    2   large tomatoes, chopped
   16   ounces angel hair pasta

In a large saucepan, sauté shrimp in olive oil, oregano, basil, pepper and garlic. Add bay scallops and continue to simmer until scallops are slightly springy to the touch. Add chicken stock. Simmer uncovered for 5 minutes on low. Remove ½ CUP chicken stock, add ½ teaspoon flour and mix thoroughly. Return to shrimp and scallop mixture. Stir and simmer uncovered for 5 minutes. Add artichokes and chopped tomatoes. Cover and simmer for 5 minutes. Prepare pasta as directed. Serve shrimp and scallop mixture over pasta.

Julie Blankenship   *4 servings*

The Italians named many of the types of pasta. "Linguine" means "tongues", "fettuccine" means "narrow ribbons", "capelli" means "angel hair."

LINGUINI WITH RED SEAFOOD SAUCE

    3   tablespoons olive oil
    1   large onion, finely chopped (1 cup)
    2   cloves of garlic, minced
    ½   cup dry white wine
    2   cups canned or homemade meatless spaghetti sauce
    2   tablespoons chopped fresh parsley
    1   bay leaf, crumbled
    2   teaspoons dried leaf basil, crumbled
    ¾   teaspoon hot sauce
    ½   teaspoon salt
    ¾   pound peeled/deveined medium shrimp
    ¾   pound sea scallops
    1   (12 ounce) package linguini, cooked according to package
        instructions

Heat oil in a 4 quart, heavy saucepan or Dutch Oven. Sauté onion and garlic over medium heat until golden brown. Add wine, simmer until reduced to 3 tablespoons. Stir in spaghetti sauce, parsley, bay leaf, basil, hot sauce and salt. Bring to a boil and add shrimp and scallops, simmering 4-5 minutes until seafood is barely firm. Toss with hot linguini in a serving bowl. Serve immediately.

Debi Barrett-Hayes   *4 servings*

SEAFOOD FETTUCCINE

    2   ounces (1 ½ cup) fettuccine
    1   teaspoon butter or margarine
    ½   cup sliced fresh mushrooms
    ¼   cup sliced green onions
    1   clove garlic, minced
    ⅔   cup milk
    3   ounces cream cheese
    2   tablespoons grated Parmesan cheese
    ¼   teaspoon dill weed
    ⅛   teaspoon pepper
    8   ounces flake style crab meat

Cook noodles according to package directions. Drain and set aside.
Melt butter in a 1 ½ quart non-stick saucepan. Sauté mushrooms, onions and garlic over low to medium heat. Stir in milk, cubed cream
cheese, Parmesan cheese, dill weed and pepper. Continue cooking,
stirring constantly, until cream cheese is melted and sauce is smooth.
Stir in crab meat and cooked noodles. Heat through.

Note: This is a perfect dish for doubling. The extra servings can be
refrigerated or frozen.

Jacqueline Singletary   2 servings

SEAFOOD LASAGNA

1 (16 ounce) package lasagna noodles
1 teaspoon olive oil
2 (10 ounce) cans Seafood Bisque or Lobster Newburg
2 (8 ounce) cans crab meat, drained
1 pint cottage cheese
8 ounces cream cheese, softened
1 medium onion, chopped
1 egg, beaten
1 teaspoon salt
2 teaspoons basil
1 cup grated mozzarella cheese
1 cup grated cheddar cheese

Prepare lasagna noodles as directed on package, adding olive oil to the water. In a large bowl, mix remaining ingredients together except cheeses. Mix together the two cheeses. In a greased 13x9 inch baking dish, layer lasagna noodles, seafood mixture, then cheese. Repeat layers twice more, ending with cheese on top. Bake in a 350° oven for 1 hour. Let stand 15 minutes before serving.

Rima Kelley

 If pasta is to be used in a dish that requires further cooking (such as lasagna), reduce pasta cooking time by one-third.

ITALIAN SURPRISE

    1 pound ground beef
    1 (16 ounce) package noodles
    ¾ cup sour cream
    1 medium onion, chopped
    1 (10 ounce) can tomatoes with chilies, drained
    1 (16 ounce) can tomato sauce
    1 (16 ounce) package Monterey Jack cheese
    ½ cup Parmesan cheese
    1 bay leaf
       salt and lemon pepper to taste

Brown ground beef and onions; drain. To meat mixture, add tomatoes, tomato sauce, bay leaves, salt and pepper. Cook noodles as directed on package; drain and mix in sour cream and lemon pepper to taste. In 9x13x2 inch casserole dish, layer, noodle mixture, meat mixture, Monterey Jack cheese and Parmesan cheese. Repeat for second layer. Bake at 350° for 30 minutes.

Nancy Sutton   *6 to 8 servings*

The best pasta is made from durum, or hard wheat. Durum has a high gluten content and makes an elastic dough which shapes easily. "Enriched" pasta is rich in B vitamins and iron.

ROMANOF BEEF NOODLE CASSEROLE

1   pound lean ground beef
1   clove garlic
1   teaspoon salt
1   (15 ounce) can tomato sauce
8   ounces fine egg noodles
½   cup cream cheese
⅔   cup sour cream
6   scallions, chopped
½   cup grated cheddar cheese
    black pepper to taste

Preheat oven to 350°. In a medium skillet sauté beef and garlic at medium heat until no pink remains in the meat. Drain fat. Add salt, pepper and tomato sauce. Simmer uncovered for 15 minutes. Meanwhile, cook noodles as package directs. Do not overcook. Drain. In a small bowl, blend cream cheese, sour cream and scallions. In a greased 2 quart casserole, place one third of the noodles, top with one third of the cream cheese mixture, then one third of the meat sauce. Repeat twice, using all ingredients. Top with cheddar cheese. (At this point you can refrigerate or freeze the casserole. Thaw before baking.) Bake at 350° for 30 minutes or until hot and bubbly.

8 servings

CHINESE NEW YEAR RICE

   3   tablespoons vegetable oil
   1   pound boneless chicken breasts, cut into bite size pieces
3 ½ cups cooked rice
   3   green onions, sliced
   1   stalk celery, diagonally sliced
   1   small carrot, grated
   2   tablespoons soy sauce
  ½ teaspoon pepper

Heat oil in large skillet or wok over medium high heat. Add chicken; cook, stirring, until lightly browned. Add remaining ingredients. Cook, stirring until heated through.

Irma S. Horn   *6 servings*

HOPPING JOHN

  2 cans blackeyed peas, drained (save liquid)
  1 cup rice
  2 teaspoons salt
  4 slices bacon, cooked, broken into pieces
  1 medium onion, chopped

Add water to juice from peas to make 2 cups of liquid. Bring to a boil. Add rice, cook over low heat, covered until rice is done. Add remaining ingredients to rice. Heat and serve.

Catherine Jessee   *6 servings*

 1 cup rice uncooked = 3 cups cooked

VENETIAN RICE AND PEAS

3 tablespoons butter
½ cup chopped onion
2 cups regular strength chicken broth
1 cup uncooked long grain rice
1 (10 ounce) package frozen green peas
½ cup diced cooked ham
salt and pepper to taste
grated Parmesan cheese

Melt butter in a large saucepan. Sauté onion in butter until transparent. Meanwhile, heat chicken broth to boiling. Add rice to onions; stir to coat with butter. Add peas, ham, salt, pepper and chicken broth; stir well. Cook, covered, over low heat about 20 minutes or until all liquid is absorbed. Sprinkle with Parmesan cheese and serve.

Sharon Piepmeier

QUICK RED BEANS AND RICE

1 pound smoked link sausage, cut into ½ inch slices
¼ cup finely chopped celery
1 medium onion, chopped
1 green pepper, chopped
1 clove garlic, minced
2 (15 ounce) cans kidney beans, drained
1 (16 ounce) can tomatoes, chopped, undrained
½ teaspoon dried whole oregano
½ teaspoon pepper
hot cooked rice

Cook sausage over low heat 5-8 minutes. Add onion, celery, green peppers, garlic, saute until tender. Drain if necessary. Add beans, tomatoes, seasonings, simmer uncovered 20 minutes. Serve over rice.

4 to 6 servings

SPANISH RICE

6 slices bacon
1 cup rice, uncooked
1 medium onion, chopped
2 cups canned tomatoes, undrained
½ teaspoon salt
1 teaspoon cumin
1 teaspoon paprika
1 green pepper, seeded and chopped
2 cloves garlic, minced
1 (14 ½ ounce) can chicken broth

Saute bacon until brown. Remove bacon, crumble, set aside. Add rice to bacon drippings and cook until brown, stirring continuously. Add onions, cook until brown. Add remaining ingredients (including bacon). Cover and cook slowly until all liquid is absorbed, about 25-30 minutes.

4 to 6 servings

"SOME LIKE IT HOT" PEPPER RICE

3 cups cooked long-grain rice
1 (8 ounce) carton sour cream
1 (4 ounce) can chopped green chilies, drained
1 medium fresh jalapeno pepper, seeded and diced
1 (8 ounce) package Monterey Jack cheese, thinly sliced
½ cup (2 ounce) shredded cheddar cheese

Combine rice, sour cream, chilies and jalapeno pepper. In a lightly greased 10x6x2 baking dish, spread ½ of rice mixture, cover with ½ of Monterey Jack cheese, then spread the rest of the rice mixture and cover with remaining Monterey Jack. Sprinkle top with cheddar cheese. Bake in a 350° oven for 15 minutes.

6 to 8 servings

RICE MIXES

LEMON DILL RICE

1 tablespoon dried grated lemon peel
1 teaspoon dried minced onion
4 chicken bouillon cubes (or 4 packets, instant chicken broth)
2 teaspoons dill weed
1 teaspoon salt
2 cups uncooked rice

VEGETABLE RICE

4 packets instant vegetable broth (or 4 vegetable bouillon cubes)
1 teaspoon salt
2 teaspoons celery seed
2 teaspoons onion flakes
2 teaspoons green pepper flakes
2 teaspoons sweet pepper flakes
2 cups uncooked rice

For either mix, combine all ingredients together. Divide the mixture into 2 portions. Store each portion in tightly closed containers. Each portion makes about 1 ¼ cups rice mix. To cook, combine 1 portion rice mix with 2 cups water and 1 tablespoon margarine in saucepan. Bring to a boil, cover tightly, cook over low heat until liquid is absorbed, about 25 minutes. Each portion makes 4-5 servings.

Hint: These mixes make excellent gifts.

PAELLA

    1   pound medium fresh shrimp, peeled and deveined
    2   chicken breasts, cooked and cut into bite size pieces
         Paella Rice Mix (see below)
2 ½ cups water

Combine Paella Rice Mix and water in a 3 quart saucepan. Bring to a boil. Cover, reduce heat, simmer 15 minutes. Stir in shrimp, cook 5 minutes. Add chicken, cook until thoroughly heated and shrimp turn pink.

4 servings

PAELLA RICE MIX

    1   (5 ounce) package saffron rice (¾ cup)
    2   tablespoons dried green onion
1 ½ teaspoons dried parsley flakes
  ½ teaspoon dried oregano
  ½ teaspoon ground cumin
  ½ teaspoon garlic powder

Combine all ingredients. Store in airtight container. Makes approximately one cup.

Vegetables

Goodwood Plantation

Goodwood Plantation was an 8,000 acre plantation for cotton, corn, and other staples during a time when the Tallahassee area was the capital of Florida's cotton kingdom. The antebellum mansion was built in 1840 by cotton baron Bryan Crooms, and modeled after an Italian villa. It featured porcelain chandeliers, brass and silver fittings, imported stained-glass windows and a cupola overlooking flourishing fields and forests. In 1910, Goodwood Plantation was bought by Fanny Tiers, known as "America's richest woman,' and the mansion was remodeled. The ornate wrought-iron porch was replaced with wooden columns, and tennis courts, guest houses, and a swimming pool were added to the property. In 1925, the house was sold to Senator William Hodges, and the mansion continued as a showplace and social center. Guests included Florida's social and political elite, students from the nearby Florida State College for Women, World War II fighter pilots from Dale Mabry Field, and children from town who came to take swimming lessons. In 1947, Thomas Hood married Hodges' widow, and upon his death in 1990, a trust fund was established to restore Goodwood Plantation's mansion and remaining nineteen acres as a museum and cultural park. Goodwood Plantation has been placed on the National Register of Historic Places.

ARTICHOKES WITH AVGOLEMONO SAUCE

    4 fresh artichokes
    3 tablespoons olive oil

SAUCE
    3 egg yolks
    3 tablespoons lemon juice
1 ¼ teaspoons arrowroot
1 ¼ cups cold chicken broth
    ½ teaspoon salt
    ¼ teaspoon white pepper

Prepare artichokes by cutting one inch directly off the top; remove any loose leaves from the bottom and cut off stem. Place upright in a deep saucepan. Cover with boiling water and olive oil; simmer for 35-45 minutes until base is tender and leaves pull off easily. While artichokes are cooking, whisk egg yolks with lemon juice, arrowroot, salt and pepper in a small saucepan. Pour chicken broth slowly into egg mixture, whisking and cooking over low heat until thickened and smooth. Use sauce for dipping artichoke leaves.

Linda Frazier   *4 servings*

Artichokes are served whole or cored and eaten as a finger food. The leaves are dipped one at a time in a sauce, and the lower end is simply pulled through the teeth to extract the tender edible portions. Then, discard the leaf.

ARTICHOKE HEARTS WITH SPINACH

    1   pound raw spinach
1-2   tablespoons butter
    1   bunch scallions, sliced (or 1 large onion, chopped)
    1   (14 ounce) can artichoke hearts
    3   slices bacon, fried and crumbled

SAUCE
    3   tablespoons butter
    6   tablespoons flour
1 ¼ cups milk
  ⅔ cup Parmesan cheese
      dash nutmeg
      salt and pepper to taste

Rinse spinach and discard tough stalks; chop coarsely. Steam spinach for several minutes until soft and limp. Melt butter; add onions and sauté until soft. Add spinach and mix thoroughly. Place artichokes in a casserole dish. Sprinkle with bacon and spinach mixture. To make sauce, in a small pan, melt butter over medium heat. Stir in flour. Slowly add milk and cook for 3 minutes, stirring occasionally. Add cheese and stir constantly until thickened. Season with nutmeg, salt and pepper. Pour sauce over vegetables and bake for 15 minutes in a 350° oven.

Judy Wheaton

When buying fresh spinach, look for bright green, fresh and tender leaves. Avoid yellowish and wilted or gritty leaves. Refrigerate either in the crisper or wrapped to avoid drying out. Use within 1-2 days.

ASPARAGUS CASSEROLE

 3 large cans asparagus pieces
 ½ cup chopped onion
 ½ cup chopped almonds or pecans
 6 hard boiled eggs, sliced
2-3 cups grated cheese
 2 (10 ¾ ounce) cans cream of mushroom soup
 ½ cup cracker crumbs

Layer asparagus, onions and nuts in a casserole dish, ending with eggs and cheese as the top layer. Pour soup over the casserole and sprinkle with cracker crumbs. Bake in a 350° oven until it is bubbly and golden brown.

Louise Jessee

SWEET AND SOUR ASPARAGUS

 ¾ cup sugar
 ¾ cup balsamic vinegar
1 ½ cups water
 3 packages unflavored gelatin
 ½ cup water
 2 tablespoons fresh lemon juice
 1 scant tablespoon salt
 1 small onion, diced
 1 small jar pimento, diced
 1 cup celery, diced
 1 can sliced water chestnuts
 2 cans cut asparagus, undrained

Combine sugar, vinegar and 1 cup water in a 2 quart saucepan; bring to a boil. Dissolve gelatin in ½ CUP water and mix with hot vinegar mixture. Cool. Add other ingredients, mixing well. Pour into a 13x9 inch pan. Chill until congealed.

Donna Peacock

CALICO BEANS

½ pound ground beef
½ pound bacon
1 large onion, chopped
½ cup ketchup
2 teaspoons salt
2 teaspoons mustard
4 teaspoons vinegar
¾ cup packed brown sugar
1 (30 ounce) can pork and beans
1 (15 ounce) can garbanzo beans, drained
1 (15 ounce) can kidney beans, drained
1 (16 ounce) package frozen lima beans, thawed with
   hot water

Brown ground beef and onion; drain. Cook bacon until crisp, crumble. Put ground beef and bacon into a 3 quart casserole dish. Add ketchup, salt, mustard, vinegar and brown sugar. Stir in all beans. Garnish with strips of bacon. Cover and bake in a 350° oven for 40 minutes or until bubbly.

Renee Howland

Soak bacon a few minutes in cold water before frying to cut down on the curling.

SPICY BAKED BEANS

   2 (16 ounce) cans pork and beans
  ½ cup spicy ketchup
  1 pound ground hot sausage
  1 can apple pie filling
  1 medium onion, chopped
  ½ green pepper, chopped
  ¼ cup brown sugar
  2 tablespoons Worcestershire sauce
  2 teaspoons prepared mustard

Brown sausage. Sauté onion and green pepper with sausage. Drain off fat. Mix together sausage mixture with remaining ingredients in a casserole dish. Bake in a 325° oven for 1 hour.

Dale Croft

GREEN BEANS WITH HERBS

  1 pound fresh green beans, cut into 1 inch pieces
  2 tablespoons margarine
  ¼ cup finely sliced celery
  2 teaspoons fresh rosemary or ½ teaspoon dried rosemary
  2 teaspoons fresh basil or ½ teaspoon dried basil
  ½ cup chopped onion
  1 clove garlic, minced

Boil or steam beans until crisp tender. Stir in remaining ingredients. Cook covered about 5 minutes or until beans are tender.

Dale Croft   *4 servings*

GREEN BEANS INDIA

  8 slices bacon
  ½ cup sugar
  ½ cup vinegar
  2 (14 ounce) cans French style green beans
  ½ medium onion, diced
  3 tablespoons India relish

Fry bacon and drain, reserving small amount of bacon drippings. Sauté onions, sugar and vinegar in reserved bacon drippings until onions are transparent. Place green beans (drained) in a 2 quart casserole and pour sugar and onion mixture over the beans. Crumble bacon and mix with relish. Top beans with this mixture and cover. Bake in a 275° oven for 1 ½ hours.

Hint: This recipe doubles easily for a large crowd. Its flavor is enhanced if it is made a day ahead, refrigerated, and then reheated before serving.

Beth Hamilton   *6 servings*

FORD-HOOK LIMA BEANS PLUS

  1 (16 ounce) package frozen lima beans
  1 (16 ounce) can French cut green beans, drained
  1 (4 ounce) jar sliced mushrooms
  1 tablespoon butter
     salt and pepper to taste

Prepare lima beans as directed on package. When done, add green beans, mushrooms, butter, salt and pepper. Add more water if desired and simmer for 10 minutes.

Mary Ann Helton   *8 to 10 servings*

BAKED LIMA BEANS

    2   cups water
    1   teaspoon salt
    1   (16 ounce) package frozen lima beans
    ½   cup celery, chopped
    ¼   cup onion, chopped
    1   cup sour cream
    ½   cup crumbled blue cheese
    4   strips bacon, fried and crumbled
        parsley to taste

Boil water and salt at medium heat in a medium saucepan. Add lima beans, celery and onion to boiling water, cooking for 12-15 minutes. Drain well in a colander, then put back into saucepan. Add sour cream and blue cheese. Place mixture in a baking dish. Sprinkle with chopped bacon and parsley. Heat in a 350° oven for 15 minutes or until bubbly.

Mickey Glenn

ORANGE BEETS

    3   cans small whole beets, drained (reserve liquid)
    2   tablespoons cornstarch
 1 ¼   cup light brown sugar
    1   (6 ounce) can frozen orange juice concentrate
    6   ounces of the drained beet liquid
    ¾   cup cider vinegar
    1   tablespoon butter

Combine cornstarch and sugar in a saucepan. Blend in orange juice concentrate followed by beet liquid and vinegar. Cook, stirring constantly until thick and clear. Add butter and beets. Keep hot until ready to serve.

Hint: This may be prepared the day before serving.

Marty Robinson

BROCCOLI CASSEROLE

2   (10 ounce) packages frozen chopped broccoli
1   cup mayonnaise
1   (10 ¾ ounce) can cream of mushroom soup
1   cup sharp cheddar cheese, grated
2   eggs, lightly beaten
    salt and pepper to taste

TOPPING
12-15   butter crackers, crushed into a fine meal
    1   stick butter, melted

Cook broccoli in water for 7 minutes; drain well. Mix all ingredients together except cracker meal and butter. Put in a large casserole dish. Sprinkle crackers over casserole. Pour butter over the top. Bake in a 350° oven for 35-40 minutes.

Linda Tinsley

BROCCOLI WITH LEMON SAUCE

1   tablespoon cornstarch
2   tablespoons cold water
½   cup water
2   tablespoons lemon juice
2   tablespoons Dijon mustard
4   cups broccoli, cut into small pieces

Steam broccoli until done. To make sauce, dissolve cornstarch in 2 tablespoons cold water. In a small saucepan, stir together ½ cup water, lemon juice and mustard. Heat ingredients and add the cornstarch mixture. Place broccoli in a serving dish and pour lemon sauce over the top.

Maria S. Shaw

BRUSSELS SPROUTS ALMANDINE

1 pound fresh brussels sprouts or
2 (10 ounce) packages frozen brussels sprouts
1 cup water
2 cubes chicken bouillon
1 (10 ¾ ounce) can cream of chicken soup
1 (2 ounce) jar pimiento, undrained
⅛ teaspoon dried whole thyme
⅛ teaspoon pepper
½ cup sliced almonds

Prepare brussels sprouts by cutting off old leaves and ends, and slashing bottoms with a shallow "X". Place brussels sprouts, water and bouillon in a medium saucepan over medium-high heat. When mixture comes to a boil, cover, reduce heat and simmer 8 minutes or until tender. Drain. Combine remaining ingredients except almonds in a 1 ½ quart casserole. Stir in brussels sprouts and sprinkle with almonds. Bake in a 350° oven for 20 minutes or until hot and bubbly.

Judy Wheaton   *8 servings*

Simple fix-ups for brussels sprouts:
* *Sprinkle cooked sprouts lightly with ground nutmeg, crushed sage, or caraway seeds.*
* *Toss cooked sprouts with butter and warm croutons.*
* *Add sliced canned water chestnuts to sprouts for added crispness.*

RED CABBAGE AND APPLES

2 pounds red cabbage, cored and shredded
1 medium onion, chopped
3 large tart green apples, peeled, cored, quartered and sliced
½ cup butter
1 teaspoon salt
2 tablespoons brown sugar
2 tablespoons cider vinegar
¼ teaspoon ground cloves
 pinch cinnamon
 pinch nutmeg
 fresh ground pepper to taste
¾ cup beer

Melt butter in a Dutch oven. Sauté cabbage, onion and apples for 10 minutes, stirring often. Add remaining ingredients; mix well. Cover and simmer 1 hour, stirring occasionally.

Hint: This dish is better if cooled and reheated.

Pat Thomas

TARRAGON CARROTS

4 peeled carrots, cut into julienne strips
½ stick butter
½ teaspoon tarragon

Melt butter in a small saucepan. Add carrots and tarragon. Cook on medium heat until carrots are tender-crisp.

Linda Frazier   *4 servings*

CREAMED CABBAGE WITH WALNUTS

   1   medium head cabbage, cored and shredded
   1   teaspoon salt
   1   cup cheddar cheese, grated
  ½   cup bread crumbs
  ½   cup walnuts, chopped

CREAM SAUCE
  ¼   cup butter
   2   tablespoons cornstarch
   1   teaspoon salt
  ¼   teaspoon pepper
   2   cups milk

Cook cabbage in 1 quart boiling water with 1 teaspoon salt for 7 minutes. Meanwhile, make cream sauce by combining butter, cornstarch, salt, pepper and milk in a saucepan on medium heat, stirring until thick. Drain cabbage. In a greased casserole, arrange in alternate layers of cabbage, walnuts, sauce and cheese, ending with layer of cheese. Sprinkle with bread crumbs. Bake in a 450° oven about 10 minutes.

Catherine Jessee   *6 to 8 servings*

All cabbage types, if fresh, are a high and inexpensive source for Vitamin C. To preserve the vitamins, keep cabbage wrapped before cooking. Use the cooked cabbage water in soups and sauces.

CARROTS AU GRATIN

    3   cups shredded carrots
   12   saltine crackers, finely crumbled
    2   tablespoons melted butter
    2   teaspoons finely minced onion
   ¼   teaspoon salt
   ½   teaspoon pepper
   ¼   cup grated cheese

Cook carrots in boiling water until tender. Drain, saving ⅔ cup liquid. Mash carrots well, stir in crumbs, butter, onion, salt and pepper. Place in a greased casserole dish; pour reserved liquid over mixture. Sprinkle with cheese. Bake in a 450° oven for 15 minutes or until cheese has melted.

Ann Blake   *6 servings*

CARROT FRITTERS

    1   bunch baby carrots, peeled
    2   eggs
    1   tablespoon sugar
    4   tablespoons flour
 1 ¼   teaspoon baking powder
        salt and pepper to taste
        corn oil (for frying)
        powdered sugar

Wash carrots, cook in a small amount of water until tender. Blend mashed carrots, eggs and sugar until creamy. Mix in flour, baking powder, salt and pepper. Spoon small amounts of batter separately into hot oil and fry until golden brown, turning once. Drain on paper towels. Sprinkle with powdered sugar while they are draining. Serve hot.

Debi Barrett-Hayes   *6 servings*

CORN CASSEROLE

 2 eggs, beaten lightly
 1 (16 ounce) can cream style corn
 1 (16 ounce) can whole kernel corn, drained
 1 (8 ½ ounce) box corn muffin mix
 1 stick butter, melted
 1 (8 ounce) carton sour cream
 8 ounces cheddar cheese, grated

Mix all ingredients together except cheese and pour into a lightly greased 2 quart casserole. Top with cheese. Bake in a 350° oven for 1 hour.

Jennifer S. Craig   *8 servings*

CORN FRITTERS

 1 (16 ounce) can whole kernel corn, drained
 1 tablespoon vegetable oil
 1 cup all-purpose flour
 1 teaspoon baking powder
 ¾ teaspoon salt
 2 eggs
 ¼ cup milk
     vegetable oil for frying

In a medium bowl, stir together ingredients just until blended. Heat about ½ inch of oil to 400°. Drop heaping tablespoonfuls of the batter into the hot oil. Fry for 3-5 minutes or until brown, turning once. With slotted spoon or spatula, remove fritters to paper towels to drain. Serve with syrup or sprinkle with confectioners sugar.

Shari Cromar

MRS. CORRELLI'S EGGPLANT CASSEROLE

2 medium eggplants, cut into ½ inch slices
¼ cup flour
  salt
2 large green peppers, cut into strips
6 ripe tomatoes, each cut into eight wedges
¼ pound bacon, cut into ½ inch pieces
1 large onion, chopped
¼ pound cheddar cheese

Salt eggplant and dredge in flour. Fry bacon; drain excess grease. Add onion and fry to a golden brown. Add tomatoes and cook until they are stewed. Place layers of eggplant, peppers, cheese and tomato mixture in a casserole dish. Bake in a 350° oven for 30 minutes.

Julia Jessee

PARMESAN EGGPLANT WITH YOGURT

1 pound eggplant
  olive oil
4 ounces feta cheese, crumbled
1 hard-boiled egg, chopped
4 tablespoons Parmesan cheese
4 tablespoons butter softened
¾ cup plain yogurt, beaten

Trim ends from eggplant and cut in half lengthwise; scoop out the seeds. Place the eggplant in a greased cooking dish and brush the cut surfaces with olive oil. Bake in a 500° oven until half done, about 15 minutes. Meanwhile, stir the feta cheese, Parmesan cheese and egg into the butter, mixing well. Remove the eggplant from the oven and reduce the heat to 350°. Stuff the cavities of the eggplant with the cheese mixture and return to the oven. Bake for 45 minutes more. Pour yogurt over the eggplant before serving.

Kathy Mitchell   *4 servings*

MUSHROOM STRUDEL

1 ½ pounds mushrooms, sliced
¼ cup butter
½ cup onions, chopped
½ teaspoon salt
¼ teaspoon white pepper
¼ teaspoon nutmeg
1 cup sour cream
¼ cup fresh parsley, chopped
½ pound phyllo dough
melted butter

Brush each sheet phyllo with melted butter and stack. Sauté mushrooms in butter with onions. Drain if too wet (this is very important). Add remaining ingredients and mix thoroughly. Unroll phyllo dough and brush butter between the sheets. Stack the sheets on top of one another. Put the mushroom mixture down the center of the dough, spreading it to about ⅓ the width of the phyllo. Fold the phyllo over toward the middle to form a strudel, folding the ends in. Brush the top with butter. Place in a greased pan and bake in a 375° oven for 45 minutes or until strudel is golden and puffy.

Hint: May be served with steak or served as an appetizer.

Linda Frazier

When sautéing mushrooms, add a teaspoon of lemon juice to each quarter pound of melted butter to keep mushrooms white and firm.

VIDALIA ONION CASSEROLE

2 large vidalia onions, sliced
2 tablespoons butter
1 can cream of corn soup (or any creamed soup)
½ cup milk
1 teaspoon soy sauce
½ loaf French bread, cut into ¾ inch slices and brushed with
      butter
2 cups Swiss cheese (or any other good melting cheese)

Sauté onions in butter. Spoon into an 8x12x2 inch casserole dish. Combine soup, milk and soy sauce and pour over onions. Sprinkle evenly with cheese. Place bread on top, buttered side up. Bake in a 350° oven for 30 minutes.

Debi Barrett-Hayes

POTATO CASSEROLE

¼ pound butter
2 cups hot milk
6 eggs
2 (12 ounce) packages frozen shredded potatoes, thawed
1 large onion, grated
   salt and pepper to taste

Add butter to hot milk. Beat eggs until frothy and add to milk. Mix in potatoes and onion. Season with salt and pepper. Put in a large casserole dish and bake in a 350° oven for 1 ½ hours.

Judy Stead Miner   *8 servings*

PEAS WITH MINT

1 ½ cups green (English) peas
2 tablespoons margarine
1 tablespoon mint leaves, chopped
1 teaspoon lemon or lime juice
   pinch of sugar
   salt and pepper to taste

Cook peas until barely tender; drain. Toss with remaining ingredients.

Nona Yaw

FRIED GREEN PEPPER RINGS

4 large green peppers
1 egg, beaten until frothy
½ cup Italian seasoned dried bread crumbs
   salt and pepper to taste
   olive oil

Rinse peppers and cut into ½ inch rings, removing centers. Dip pepper rings in egg then roll in bread crumbs. Fry in oil until golden brown.

Brunetta Pfaender   *8 servings*

As fried foods are removed from the oil, place in paper bags to drain. It will help soak up excess oils.

STUFFED POTATOES WITH CRAB MEAT

10 medium potatoes
1 cup milk or half and half
2 sticks butter
½ cup sour cream
¾ cup finely chopped green onions
¼ cup chopped parsley
½ cup bacon bits
¾ pound white crab meat
1 cup cheese of your choice, grated
  salt and pepper to taste

Clean potatoes. Bake or micro-cook potatoes. Cool just enough to handle. Cut potatoes lengthwise and scoop out, reserving shells. Mash potatoes with milk, butter and sour cream. Add onions, parsley, bacon bits, crab meat, salt and pepper, mixing thoroughly. Scoop back into potato shells. Top with cheese. Bake in a 350° oven for 20-25 minutes until cheese melts and potatoes start to brown.

Debi Barrett-Hayes

A green tinge on a potato indicates the presence of solanin, which can cause sickness if enough of it is eaten. Peel the potato, removing all the green tinge.

CRISPY POTATO WEDGES

¼ cup olive oil
½ teaspoon salt
¼ teaspoon black pepper
½ teaspoon dried parsley
½ teaspoon dill weed
½ teaspoon garlic salt
½ teaspoon dried basil
4-6 medium potatoes, unpeeled and scrubbed
¼-½ cup grated Parmesan cheese

Combine all ingredients except potatoes and Parmesan cheese in a bowl. Scrub unpeeled potatoes well. Cut each potato in half lengthwise, then into thirds (6 wedges per potato). Coat each wedge in seasoned oil. Spread in a single layer on a greased baking sheet. Bake in a 450° oven for 15 minutes. Sprinkle with cheese and bake 15 minutes longer.

Nona Yaw   *4 servings*

 Store potatoes in a dark, cool and dry place. Do not refrigerate as the starch will convert to sugar, changing the flavor.

APRICOT-GLAZED SWEET POTATOES

3 pounds sweet potatoes, cooked, peeled and cut up
1 cup packed brown sugar
5 teaspoons cornstarch
¼ teaspoon salt
⅛ teaspoon ground cinnamon
1 cup apricot nectar
½ cup hot water
2 teaspoons grated orange peel
2 teaspoons butter or margarine
½ cup chopped pecans

Place sweet potatoes in a 13x9x2 inch baking dish and set aside. In a saucepan, combine sugar, cornstarch, salt and cinnamon; stir in apricot nectar, water and orange peel. Bring to a boil, stirring constantly. Cook and stir 2 minutes more. Remove from heat; stir in butter and pecans. Pour over sweet potatoes. Bake uncovered in a 350° oven for 20-25 minutes or until heated through.

Nona Yaw   *8 servings*

For simple peeling, take sweet potatoes from boiling water and plunge immediately into cold water. The skin will fall off.

SPINACH CASSEROLE

3 (10 ounce) packages frozen chopped spinach
½ cup butter, softened
1 (8 ounce) package cream cheese, softened
1 egg
1 onion, diced
1 tablespoon milk
¼ cup lemon juice
1 cup grated cheddar cheese
  salt and pepper to taste

Cook spinach according to package directions; drain. Cream together butter and cream cheese. Add all remaining ingredients except cheddar cheese and mix well. Turn into a casserole dish. Top with cheese and bake in a 350° oven until bubbly, about 15 minutes.

Nona Yaw   *8 servings*

SQUASH-TOMATO CASSEROLE

4 medium yellow squash, sliced very thin lengthwise
1 large onion, sliced and separated into rings
2 medium tomatoes, sliced
  seasoned salt, salt and pepper to taste
4 slices bacon, cut into pieces
1 cup grated cheddar cheese

Place 3-4 layers of squash on bottom of a 13x9 inch baking dish. Add a layer of onion rings followed by a layer of tomatoes. Sprinkle with seasoning salt, salt and pepper. Top with cheese. Add a layer of bacon. Bake in a 350° oven for 30-45 minutes until vegetables are tender.

Thelma Hartsfield

ZUCCHINI WITH ALMONDS

½ cup chopped onion
1 tablespoon water
⅛ teaspoon salt
2 cups zucchini, sliced ¼ inch thick
2 tablespoons sliced almonds, toasted
2 teaspoons butter or margarine
½ teaspoon dried marjoram, crushed
½ teaspoon lemon juice
  pepper to taste
2 tablespoons grated Parmesan cheese

Combine onion, water and salt in a 1 ½ quart microwave-safe casserole. Micro-cook on HIGH for 2 minutes. Stir in zucchini. Micro-cook, covered, on HIGH for 3-5 minutes or until zucchini is tender-crisp, stirring once. Drain. Stir in the almonds, butter, marjoram, lemon juice and pepper. Micro-cook, covered, on HIGH for 30-60 seconds or until the mixture is heated through. Sprinkle with Parmesan cheese.

Diana Johnson   *4 servings*

 Once an onion has been cut into half, rub the leftover cut side with butter to keep it fresh longer.

ZUCCHINI "DON'T EVEN KNOW IT'S A VEGGIE" CASSEROLE

    3   cups zucchini, cut into small pieces
    ¼   cup sour cream
    1   tablespoon butter or margarine
    1   tablespoon grated Parmesan cheese
    ½   teaspoon salt
    ⅛   teaspoon paprika
    1   egg yolk, beaten
    1   tablespoon chopped chives
    ¼   cup bread crumbs

Simmer zucchini in a covered steamer for 6-8 minutes until so tender it loses its shape. Drain. Combine sour cream, butter, cheese, salt and paprika. Stir mixture into zucchini over low heat until cheese is melted. Remove from heat and stir in egg yolk and chives. Place mixture into a greased baking dish and top with bread crumbs. Bake in a 375° oven for 10 minutes.

Candy Mitchell   *4 servings*

To prevent sour cream from curdling when adding to a hot mixture, bring to room temperature first. When heating a dish with sour cream, stir often and remove from heat before it can boil.

STUFFED ZUCCHINI

  7 medium zucchini
  3 tablespoons olive oil
  1 clove garlic, crushed
  ½ cup fresh parsley, chopped
  1 tablespoon fresh marjoram, or ½ teaspoon dried
  1 small onion, finely chopped
  ¼ pound mushrooms, chopped
  ¾ cup whole-wheat bread crumbs
  ¼ cup milk
  ⅔ cup freshly grated Parmesan cheese
  1 egg, beaten
     salt and pepper to taste
  2 tablespoons butter

Steam zucchini for 10 minutes or until just tender. Cool slightly. Cut lengthwise into halves and scoop out, leaving shells ¼ inch thick. Chop what was scooped out.

Heat the oil in a skillet and sauté garlic, parsley and marjoram for 1 minute. Add onion and cook over medium heat for 5 minutes. Add chopped zucchini and mushrooms and continue to cook until tender and turning golden. Soak bread crumbs in milk. Place onion mixture, bread crumbs, ⅓ cup Parmesan cheese, egg, salt and pepper in a bowl and mix well.

Stuff the zucchini shells with the mixture. Sprinkle with remaining cheese and dot with butter. Arrange side by side on a well-oiled baking sheet. Bake in a 350° oven for 30 minutes or until tops are golden.

Kathy Mitchell   *4 to 6 servings*

DEVILED TOMATOES

    4 firm tomatoes
    2 tablespoons butter or margarine
    1 small clove garlic, crushed
    ½ cup fresh bread crumbs
    3 tablespoons chopped fresh parsley
    ¼ teaspoon cayenne pepper
    ½ teaspoon paprika
    ¼ teaspoon dry mustard
    1 tablespoon grated Parmesan cheese
       salt to taste

Cut a ⅓ inch slice off of the top of each tomato. Reserve tops. Remove seeds from each tomato. Melt butter in a saucepan. Add garlic, bread crumbs and parsley, mixing well. Remove from heat. Add cayenne pepper, paprika, mustard, cheese and salt, mixing well. Spoon into tomatoes and form into neat mounds, pressing gently in shape with fingertips. Put reserved lids on top. Arrange tomatoes, cut sides up, in a greased pan. Bake in a 350° oven for 15 minutes. Garnish with parsley sprigs; serve hot.

Debi Barrett-Hayes   *4 servings*

FRIED GREEN TOMATOES

    2 firm green tomatoes, sliced ¼-½ inch thick
    1 cup corn meal
       salt to taste
       dash sugar
       cooking oil (or bacon drippings)

Mix corn meal, salt and sugar. Dip tomato slices into corn meal. Fry tomatoes in oil until brown, turning once. Remove from oil and drain on paper towels. Serve hot.

Ann Boyd   *4 servings*

VEGETABLE MIX-UP

1 ½ cups broccoli florets
1 cup carrots, angle-sliced, ⅛ inch thick
1 cup celery, angle-sliced, ⅜ inch thick
1 cup zucchini, angle-sliced, ⅜ inch thick
1 cup fresh mushrooms, sliced, ⅜ inch thick
1 medium onion, cut into 8 wedges
2 tablespoons water
3 tablespoons butter or margarine, softened
1 tablespoon lemon juice
¾ teaspoon dried basil, crushed
½ teaspoon salt (optional)
¼ teaspoon dried thyme, crushed
⅛ teaspoon pepper
¼ cup grated Parmesan cheese

In a 2 quart casserole dish, combine all vegetables and water. Bake, covered, in a 375° oven for 40-45 minutes. Drain. Add all remaining ingredients except cheese and stir to coat. Sprinkle with cheese. Bake, uncovered, 5 minutes or until cheese is melted.

Microwave directions: Micro-cook vegetables with water, covered but vented, on HIGH for 8-10 minutes, stirring every 4 minutes. Drain. Add all remaining ingredients except cheese and stir to coat. Sprinkle with cheese. Micro-cook, uncovered, on HIGH for 1 ½-2 minutes.

Kim Cooper   *6 to 8 servings*

Accompaniments

Black Archives Research Center and Museum

The Black Archives Research Center and Museum is located in the oldest building on the Florida Agricultural and Mechanical University campus. The building was completed in 1907 with the assistance of a grant from Andrew Carnegie and has been placed on the National Register of Historic Places.

The Black Archives Research Center and Museum was established in 1971 for the purpose of serving as a repository to collect and preserve source material about African Americans. It contains an extensive collection of African American artifacts, a five hundred piece Ethiopian cross collection, and memorabilia of notable African American heroes. The Museum is also dedicated to preserving the strong oral history of the African American culture and maintains an oral history laboratory which provides a record of race relations and customs in the South.

BLACK BEAN STUFFING

1	pound bulk pork sausage
1	cup onion, chopped
1	cup celery, sliced
1	(15 ounce) can black beans, drained
1	(12 ounce) can whole kernel corn, drained
8	ounces fresh mushrooms, chopped (about 3 cups)
½	cup fresh parsley, chopped
¼	cup butter, melted
1	teaspoon dried sage
1	teaspoon pepper
5	cups coarsely crumbled corn bread
½-¾	cup chicken broth

In a large skillet, cook sausage, onion and celery until sausage is brown and onion is tender; drain. In a large bowl combine sausage mixture, beans, corn, mushrooms, parsley, butter, sage and pepper. Stir in corn bread. Drizzle with enough chicken broth to moisten, tossing until mixed. Bake, covered, in a 4 quart casserole dish in a 375° oven for 45 minutes.

Brunetta Pfaender   *12 cups*

To measure soft bread crumbs, pile lightly into a cup (do not pack down). Use promptly, before they dry out. When making crumbs, use a fork instead of tearing bread with the hands to avoid crushing.

CORN STUFFING

1   (17 ounce) can cream-style corn
2   (4 ounce) cans chopped green chili peppers, drained
1   (4 ½ ounce) can chopped ripe olives
¾   cup Monterey Jack cheese, grated
½   cup finely chopped onion
½   cup chopped green pepper
1   tablespoon fresh cilantro or parsley, chopped
1   egg, beaten
6   cups crumbled corn bread

In a large bowl combine all ingredients except corn bread, mixing well. Add corn bread; toss to mix. Bake, covered, in a 2 quart casserole dish in a 325° oven for 45 minutes.

Brunetta Pfaender   *8 to 10 servings*

WILD RICE STUFFING

½   cup raw wild rice
    giblets
1   tablespoon butter
1   small onion, chopped
¼   pound bulk sausage
1   teaspoon salt
½   teaspoon dried sage

Soak rice overnight in enough cold water to cover. Drain water and put rice in a double boiler; cover and steam for 10 minutes. Clean, wash and chop giblets. Melt butter and sauté giblets, onion and sausage for 10 minutes. Add cooked rice, salt and sage; cook 2 minutes longer. Bake, covered, in a 350° oven for 30 minutes.

PAUL'S TURKEY DRESSING

    1   pound hot bulk sausage
    ½   cup butter
    ½   cup finely chopped celery
    2   cups corn bread (1 small prepared package)
    4   cups toasted bread, cubed
    ¾   cup finely chopped onion
    2   eggs, beaten
    1   teaspoon poultry seasoning
    ¼   teaspoon salt
  1/8   teaspoon pepper

Cook sausage well, breaking up with spoon; drain. Cook celery in butter until clear. Mix all ingredients. Put into a casserole dish and bake in a 350° oven for 30 minutes.

Jane Love   *2 quarts*

APRICOT DRESSING

  2 ½   cups cooked, unsweetened apricots
    2   cups soft bread crumbs
    2   cups cracker crumbs
    ¼   cup butter, melted
    ¼   cup minced celery
    ½   cup almonds, chopped
  1 ½   teaspoons salt
        pepper to taste

Cut apricots in small pieces. Add remaining ingredients, mixing well. Bake in a 400° oven for about 20 minutes or until top browns.

BREAD DRESSING

4 cups bread, cubed
  milk or hot water to moisten
1 teaspoon salt
¼ teaspoon pepper
¼ teaspoon poultry seasoning
1 egg, slightly beaten
3 tablespoons butter
3 tablespoons chopped onion

Moisten bread with milk or water. Add salt, pepper, poultry seasoning and egg to bread. Melt butter. Add onion, simmer slightly and
add to dressing. Mix gently. Bake in a 400° oven for about 20 minutes
or until top browns.

Variations:
CELERY DRESSING: Add 1 ½ cups chopped celery to bread dressing.

GIBLET DRESSING: Add chopped, cooked giblets to bread dressing.

OYSTER DRESSING: Heat 1 ½ cups oysters in 2 tablespoons butter
and add to bread dressing.

CORNBREAD DRESSING: Substitute 4 cups of day old cornbread
and add at least one (14 ounce) can of chicken soup.

GIBLET GRAVY

    giblets, neck, tips of wings
2 ½ cups salted water
  4 tablespoons flour
  2 tablespoons fat

Simmer giblets and other parts in salted water. Remove giblets; chop
fine. Brown flour in fat. Add 2 cups stock from giblets; simmer, stirring constantly until thick. Add giblets and cook 5 more minutes.

SAUERKRAUT RELISH

½ cup sugar
½ cup vinegar
1 (16 ounce) can sauerkraut
1 cup diced celery
1 cup diced green pepper
1 cup chopped onion
1 (2 ounce) jar chopped pimiento

Heat vinegar and sugar until dissolved; cool. Combine undrained sauerkraut, celery, green pepper, onion and drained pimiento; add to vinegar mixture. Chill. Good on hotdogs and other meats.

Mary D. Beasley

HAM GLAZE

¾ cup bourbon
3 tablespoons butter, melted and cooled
3 cups dark brown sugar
¼ teaspoon coriander
1 tablespoon dry mustard
3 tablespoons orange marmalade
  cloves

Mix all ingredients together except cloves. One hour before ham is done, glaze and stud ham with cloves; continue baking. Baste every 15 minutes.

Pat Thomas

STEAK MARINADE

> 1 cup soy sauce
> 1 tablespoon olive oil
> 1 clove garlic, crushed
> 1 teaspoon ginger
> 1 small onion, finely chopped
> ½ cup red wine

Combine all ingredients. Marinade steaks in mixture for several hours.

Brunetta Pfaender

TURKEY BASTING MARINADE

Melt ½ cup butter in saucepan; add 1 cup orange juice, ½ cup lemon juice and ¼ teaspoon rosemary.   OR

Melt ½ cup butter in saucepan; add 1 cup apple juice, ½ cup lemon juice and ¼ teaspoon tarragon.

MARINADE FOR GAME

Combine equal parts hearty burgundy and dry Italian dressing. Mix well. Use marinade with any dark meat before grilling.

Alan Schweitzer

MARINADE FOR DOMESTIC MEAT, GAME OR FOWL

1 ½   cups red wine (not too sweet)
¾   cup red wine vinegar
1   medium onion, coarsely chopped
1   carrot, cut into chunks
2   celery stalks, cut into chunks
1   clove garlic, minced
½   teaspoon dill weed or dill seeds
½   teaspoon mustard seeds
½   teaspoon coriander, bruised
6   juniper seeds (optional)
½   teaspoon pepper corns, crushed
½   teaspoon thyme
½   teaspoon rosemary
½   teaspoon celery seed
½   teaspoon caraway seed (optional)
¾   cup water

Mix all together ingredients in a large bowl. Place meat in a marinade container and pour marinade over meat to cover. (If marinade does not cover meat, more water may be added.) Refrigerate. Turn meat at least twice a day. Meat may marinade for up to 3 days.

Hint: The left over marinade may be brought to a boil, cooled, strained and used to season stock or gravy.

Avenell R. Tate

EASY BARBECUE SAUCE

    2   tablespoons sugar
    2   tablespoons vinegar
    2   tablespoons Worcestershire sauce
    ¾   cup ketchup, filled to a cup with water

Mix all ingredients well. Use when grilling chicken or hamburgers. Also good served over ham.

Variation:
BARBECUE BAKED BEANS: Mix sauce with a large can of pork and beans. Bake in a 350° oven for 30 minutes.

D.J. Matthias

COCKTAIL SAUCE

    1   cup ketchup
    2   tablespoons Worcestershire sauce
    2   tablespoons lemon juice
    1   teaspoon hot sauce
    2   tablespoons prepared horseradish

Combine all ingredients.

Brunetta Pfaender

CREAM SAUCE

- 2 tablespoons butter
- 2 tablespoons flour
- 1 cup milk
  salt to taste

Melt butter in saucepan. Gradually add flour, stirring until smooth. Gradually add milk; cook on medium heat until thickened, stirring constantly.

Hint: This sauce can be used for vegetables, creamed chicken, turkey, tuna or chipped beef.

Variations:
CREAMED CHICKEN, TURKEY, TUNA OR CHIPPED BEEF: Add meat. Serve on toast.

ASPARAGUS IN CHEESE SAUCE: Add to asparagus and cheese.

Katherine Jessee

TARTAR SAUCE

- ⅔ cup mayonnaise
- 3 tablespoons sweet pickle relish
- 2 tablespoons green olives
- 1 tablespoon parsley
- 1 tablespoon finely chopped onion
- 1 teaspoon prepared horseradish (optional)

Blend all ingredients together; cover and chill.

Brunetta Pfaender   *1 cup*

ROASTED SWEET PEPPERS

  1 yellow pepper, whole
  1 bell pepper, whole
  1 red pepper, whole
  1 medium onion, finely chopped
  ⅓ cup corn or vegetable oil
  2 tablespoons lemon juice
  1 teaspoon coarsely ground dry mustard
  1 clove garlic
  ½ teaspoon sugar
     salt and pepper to taste

Place peppers, stem side down, in roasting pan. Bake in a 400° oven for 30 minutes or until skins begin to blister and blacken. Cool, then peel skins. Cut peppers into fourths and slice into strips. Put peppers into a shallow dish. Sprinkle with onion. Combine remaining ingredients in a screw top jar and shake. Pour over pepper and onions. Marinate overnight.

Hint: This keeps for three days in the refrigerator. Serve with meats, breads, crackers and cheeses.

Debi Barrett-Hayes

MAPLE CANDIED APPLES

  2 medium apples, cored and cut into 8 wedges
  ¼ cup apple juice
  ¼ cup maple flavored syrup
  1 tablespoon butter, melted

Place apples in a 1 quart microwave-safe dish. Combine remaining ingredients; pour over apples. Cover and micro-cook on HIGH for 3-5 minutes or until apples are tender.

Kim Cooper   *4 servings*

APPLE SCALLOP

 6 baking apples, peeled, cored and sliced into rings
 ½ cup sugar
   grated rind of 1 orange
 ¼ cup butter, melted
 ½ teaspoon salt
   dash ground ginger
   dash nutmeg
   dash ground cloves
3-4 drops almond extract
 ⅓ cup orange juice

Place apple rings into a 13x9 inch baking pan. Combine remaining ingredients and pour over apples. Bake, covered, in a 350° oven for 50 minutes.

Hint: This dish is very good with pork.

Pat Thomas   *6 to 8 servings*

SPICED BLUEBERRIES

 2 quarts blueberries
 ½ cup vinegar
 1 teaspoon cinnamon
 ½ teaspoon ground cloves
 2 cups sugar

Wash berries, add vinegar and spices and boil for ½ hour. Add sugar and boil ½ hour longer or until thickened, stirring occasionally to prevent scorching. Pour into sterilized jars and seal.

Hint: Serve over pancakes or ice cream.

Pat Thomas   *2 pints*

CRANBERRY RELISH

    1   quart cranberries
    1   large seedless orange
    4   medium apples
    4   cups sugar

Peel orange. Peel and core apples. Grind up all fruit with a fine cutter. Add sugar, stir well. Let set in refrigerator at least 24 hours before serving.

Cindy Mackiernan

AMBROSIA

    3   oranges, peeled and chopped
    2   grapefruit, peeled and chopped
    2   apples, cored and chopped
    2   bananas, peeled and sliced
    ¾   cup coconut
    ½   cup pecans, chopped
        sugar to taste

Mix all ingredients and refrigerate until ready to serve.

Variation: Substitute artificial sweetener or orange-flavored liqueur for the sugar.

Hazel Pfaender

FRUIT COMPOTE

    1   pint strawberries, sliced
        light brown sugar
        green grapes, cut
        bananas, sliced
        sour cream

In a glass bowl layer sliced strawberries. Sprinkle with brown sugar. Add a layer of grapes and bananas, covering with a layer of sour cream. Repeat layers to fill bowl, finishing with sour cream. Refrigerate for several hours. Serve in a sherbet dish or small glass bowl.

Hint: This is an easy dish that is attractive for special occasions; especially good for breakfast or brunch.

Vilma Wollschlager

HOT FRUIT COMPOTE

       1   (16 ounce) can sliced pears packed in juice, drained
       1   (16 ounce) can sliced peaches packed in juice, drained
       1   (8 ounce) can pineapple chunks packed in juice, drained
    1 ½   cups unsweetened applesauce
   ¼ -½   cup raisins (optional)
       ½   teaspoon cinnamon
       ¼   teaspoon nutmeg
       ⅛   teaspoon allspice
       ¼   cup firmly packed brown sugar
       2   tablespoons orange-flavored liqueur (optional)

Combine all ingredients in a large saucepan, mixing well; heat until warm.

Hint: This dish is also very good cold.

Pat Thomas   *8 servings*

MAI TAI COMPOTE

1   medium fresh pineapple
1   orange, peeled and sliced
1   kiwi, peeled and sliced
1   cup strawberries, halved
½   cup seedless red grapes
¼   cup fresh lime juice
3   tablespoons honey
1   tablespoon light rum (or 1 teaspoon rum extract)
1   tablespoon orange-flavored liqueur (or orange juice)
½   teaspoon grated lime peel
1   firm banana, peeled and sliced

Cut pineapple in half lengthwise through the crown. Remove fruit, leaving shells intact. Core and chunk pineapple. Mix pineapple with orange, kiwi, berries and grapes. Combine remaining ingredients except bananas. Pour over fruit. Toss gently to coat. Marinate 1 hour. Add bananas just before serving. Toss. Spoon fruit into pineapple shells to serve.

Nona Yaw   *6 to 8 servings*

SPICED PEACHES

1   (16 ounce) can peach slices in heavy syrup
2   teaspoons vinegar
½   teaspoon cinnamon
¼   teaspoon whole cloves

Drain peaches, reserving liquid. Place peaches in a 1 quart microwave-safe dish. Combine syrup, vinegar, cinnamon and cloves; pour over peaches. Micro-cook on HIGH, uncovered, for 5 minutes.

Kim Cooper   *4 servings*

CURRIED FRUIT

1 (16 ounce) can peaches, drained
1 (16 ounce) can pears, drained
1 (16 ounce) can apricots, drained
1 (16 ounce) can cherries, drained
1 (20 ounce) can chunk pineapple, drained
1 cup brown sugar
1 stick butter
2 tablespoons curry powder
1 jar maraschino cherries

Layer fruit in a 2 quart casserole dish. Heat sugar, margarine and curry powder in a saucepan until butter is melted. Pour over fruit. Top with maraschino cherries in juice. Bake in a 350° oven for 1 hour. Serve warm.

6 servings

SCALLOPED PINEAPPLE

1 (20 ounce) can pineapple chunks, drained
4 cups fresh breadcrumbs
3 eggs beaten
2 cups sugar
1 cup butter, melted

Mix pineapple and breadcrumbs, placed in a greased 2 quart baking dish. Combine remaining ingredients and pour over pineapple. Bake at 350° for 30 minutes. Can be refrigerated overnight before cooking.

Beth Hamilton   *6 to 8 servings*

CRANBERRY-SPICED PEARS

⅔ cup cranberry juice cocktail
½-1 teaspoon cinnamon (to taste)
4 small pears, peeled, halved and cored (or 1 (16 ounce) can pear halves, drained)

In a 1 quart microwave-safe dish, combine juice and cinnamon. Place pears, cut side down, in sauce, arranging in a circle. Spoon sauce over pears. Micro-cook, covered, on HIGH for 9-10 minutes or until pears are tender (2 ½ -3 ½ minutes for canned pears). Spoon sauce over pears again before serving.

Kim Cooper   *4 servings*

HONEYED STRAWBERRIES AND BANANAS

1 cup strawberries, halved
1 large banana, sliced
⅓ cup plain yogurt
2 tablespoons honey

Mix all ingredients and serve immediately.

Brunetta Pfaender

Desserts

Florida State University

The Florida State University had its beginning in 1823 when the Territorial Legislature began to plan a system for higher education. In 1851, the Florida Legislature established two seminaries, one on either side of the Suwannee River, and in 1855, Tallahassee was chosen as the site of the western seminary. In 1857, the Seminary West of the Suwannee River, or the West Florida Seminary as it was later known, began offering postsecondary instruction to male students. It was located on a hill where the Westcott Building now stands. Subsequently, the school became coeducational. In 1863, the name was changed to the Florida Military and Collegiate Institute to reflect the addition of a military training program for cadets.

By 1897, the Institute had evolved into the first liberal arts college in Florida, and in 1901, it was renamed Florida State College. With a legislative reorganization of the higher education system in 1905, the Florida State College became a women's school called the Florida Female College. The name was later changed to the Florida State College for Women and by the 1930's the college had become the third largest women's college in the nation. In 1947, the return of World War II veterans caused the Legislature to once again designate the college as coeducational and to rename it The Florida State University.

Today, The Florida State University (FSU) maintains comprehensive and graduate level curriculums. It is a major research institution with a renowned international reputation due in part to its acquisition of a magnetic field laboratory and supercomputer. In addition, FSU's athletic teams in football, basketball, and baseball have repeatedly enjoyed national prominence. Similarity, the FSU Flying High Circus is the most prestigious collegiate circus in the nation.

HUMMINGBIRD CAKE

CAKE

 3 cups all-purpose flour
 2 cups sugar
 1 teaspoon salt
 1 teaspoon baking soda
 1 teaspoon cinnamon
 3 eggs, beaten
1 ½ cups cooking oil
1 ½ teaspoons vanilla extract
 1 (8 ounce) can crushed pineapple in juice (do not drain)
 2 cups chopped nuts (pecans)
 2 cups mashed bananas

CREAM CHEESE FROSTING

 2 (8 ounce) packages cream cheese, softened
 1 cup margarine
 2 (16 ounce) packages powdered sugar
 2 teaspoons vanilla

Blend together dry cake ingredients. Add eggs and oil. Fold in vanilla, pineapple and juice, nuts and bananas. Pour into either three 9 inch cake pans, or a bundt pan, greased and floured. Bake in a 350° oven for 25-30 minutes for cake pans or 45-60 minutes for bundt pan. To prepare frosting, combine cream cheese and margarine; blend in sugar and vanilla. Frost cake when cool.

Gail Sloane

BLENDER CARROT CAKE

CAKE

1 ¼	cups salad oil
4	eggs
2	cups sugar
2	teaspoons cinnamon
1	teaspoon salt
3	cups sliced raw carrots
2	cups flour
1	teaspoon baking soda
2	teaspoons baking powder
1	teaspoon cloves
½	teaspoon nutmeg
1	cup chopped pecans

FROSTING

4	tablespoons butter
1	(8 ounce) package cream cheese, softened
2	cups confectioners sugar, sifted
1	teaspoon vanilla
½	cup chopped pecans

Combine first five ingredients in blender and blend for 5 seconds. Add carrots and blend until grated. Sift remaining cake ingredients, except pecans, together in a large bowl. Pour blender contents over dry ingredients; mix well. Stir in pecans. Pour into a greased tube pan. Bake in a 325° oven for 1 hour and 10 minutes. Blend frosting ingredients in order. Frost cake when completely cool. Refrigerate cake after frosting.

Donna Peacock   *12 servings*

NANNIE'S CAKE

CAKE
- 1 cup butter (2 sticks)
- 2 cups sugar
- 3 cups cake flour
- ½ teaspoon salt
- 4 eggs
- 3 teaspoons baking powder
- 4 ripe bananas
- 2 teaspoons vanilla
- 1 cup pecan pieces

TOPPING
- ¾ stick butter, room temperature
- 1 cup shredded coconut
- ½ cup pecan pieces
- ½ cup sugar
- 1 teaspoon vanilla

Cream butter and sugar until fluffy. Add eggs one at a time, beating mixture after each egg. Puree bananas in blender and add to mixture. Add flour, baking powder, salt and vanilla; mix well. Grease a bundt pan or 9x13 inch pan with a solid shortening (DO NOT USE OIL). Dust bottom of pan with flour, and pour in batter. Bake in a preheated 325° oven. Due to varying pan sizes, check after 30 minutes by sticking a toothpick into the center. When the toothpick comes out clean, the cake is done. Thoroughly mix all topping ingredients together. Add to cake as soon as it comes out of oven. Return immediately to oven to brown topping. This should only take a few minutes. Place a flat pan of water on bottom rack of oven to keep the bottom of cake from burning.

Ann Boyd

SOUR CREAM COFFEE CAKE

CAKE
- 2 cups flour
- 3 teaspoons baking powder
- 1 teaspoon baking soda
- 1 cup sugar
- ½ cup butter or margarine
- 2 eggs
- 2 teaspoons vanilla
- 1 ½ cups sour cream

CINNAMON MIXTURE
- 2 tablespoons cinnamon
- ½ cup sugar
- ½ cup chopped pecans

Mix cake ingredients thoroughly. Pour ½ of mixture into greased and floured bundt pan. Sprinkle with ½ of cinnamon mixture; stir into cake with a spoon. Repeat with second half of cake mixture. Bake in a 350° oven for 30-35 minutes.

Sharon Cromar

MICHIGAN POUND CAKE

- 2 sticks butter
- 3 cups sugar
- 6 eggs
- 3 cups cake flour
- 1 cup whipping cream
- 1 teaspoon vanilla or rum flavoring

Cream butter and sugar. Beat in eggs one at a time. Add flour, cream and vanilla, beating until smooth. Pour batter into a greased bundt pan. Bake in a 275° oven for 1 ½ hours.

Catherine Robinson

CHOCOLATE SOUR CREAM POUND CAKE

     3 sticks butter or margarine (room temperature)
     3 cups sugar
     5 eggs
    ½ cup cocoa
     3 cups all-purpose flour
     1 teaspoon baking soda
    ¼ teaspoon salt
     1 (8 ounce) carton sour cream
     1 cup boiling water
  1 ½ teaspoons vanilla

Preheat oven to 325°. Cream butter; gradually add sugar. Add eggs one at a time. Mix together all dry ingredients. Gradually add dry ingredients to sugar/butter mixture, alternating with sour cream. Add water and vanilla. Mix. Pour batter into greased and floured 10 inch tube or bundt pan. Bake for 1 ½ hours or until cake tests done. Cool cake for about 10 minutes in pan; remove from pan to cool further.

Cynthia B. Johnson   *10 to 12 servings*

4 BANANA POUND CAKE

     1 package yellow cake mix
     4 eggs
    ⅓ cup oil
    ½ cup water
  1 ⅓ cups mashed ripe bananas (4 medium size)
     1 small box instant vanilla pudding mix
    ½ teaspoon cinnamon
    ½ teaspoon nutmeg

Combine all ingredients in a large bowl; blend well. Pour into a greased and floured 10 inch tube pan. Bake in a 350° oven for 1 hour, test with a toothpick. Cool 10 minutes in pan. Remove from pan and dust with powdered sugar.

Sally Baker

HARVEST PUMPKIN CHEESECAKE

CRUST

¼ cup graham cracker crumbs
½ cup pecans, finely chopped
¼ cup light brown sugar, firmly packed
¼ cup sugar
½ stick unsalted butter, melted and cooled

FILLING

32 ounces cream cheese, softened
1 ½ cups sugar
5 large eggs
¼ cup flour
¼ teaspoon salt
1 (16 ounce) can pumpkin
2 teaspoons cinnamon
2 teaspoons ginger
2 teaspoons nutmeg
1 tablespoon bourbon

TOPPING

2 cups sour cream
¼ cup sugar
1 tablespoon bourbon
16 pecan halves

In a medium bowl, combine cracker crumbs, pecans and sugars. Stir in butter. Press mixture into bottom and ½ inch up sides of lightly greased 9 inch spring form pan. Chill 1 hour or over night. Preheat oven to 325°. In a large bowl, beat cream cheese until fluffy. Gradually add sugar. Add eggs one at a time, beating after each one. Beat in remaining ingredients; pour into chilled crust. Bake 1 ½ hours. Should be firm around edges, but still soft in center. Remove from oven, cool for 5 minutes. Leave oven on. To make topping, in a medium bowl, whisk together sour cream, sugar and bourbon. Spread mixture on top of cake and bake 5 minutes more. Cool in pan. Cover and refrigerate overnight. Garnish with pecans.

Candy Mitchell

APPLESAUCE FRUIT CAKE

   4 eggs
   2 sticks margarine, room temperature
   2 cups sugar
   3 cups flour
   1 teaspoon baking soda
   1 teaspoon salt
   1 teaspoon cinnamon
   1 cup applesauce
   2 cups nuts, chopped fine
   2 cups candied pineapple
   1 pound candied cherries

Cream margarine and sugar. Add eggs one at a time, beating well after each addition. Add dry ingredients alternately with applesauce. Fold in nuts, pineapples and cherries. Pour into a tube pan. Bake in a 250° oven for 2 ½ hours.

Kittie Mae Grant

Toss nuts and candied fruit in about ½ cup of flour (to coat them) before adding to fruitcake. They won't sink to the bottom of the batter.

LEMONADE CAKE

CAKE
 1   small package lemon gelatin
 ¾ cup boiling water
 4 eggs
 ¾ cup cooking oil
 1   package yellow cake mix

GLAZE
 1   small can lemonade concentrate
 ½ cup sugar

Dissolve lemon gelatin in boiling water. Let cool. In a large mixing bowl, beat eggs thoroughly. Add cooking oil. Alternately add cake mix and dissolved lemon gelatin mixture. Pour into a tube pan. Bake in a 350° oven for 1 hour. To prepare glaze, dissolve sugar in heated lemon concentrate. Remove cake from oven and leave in cake pan to glaze. Leave in pan 1 hour before removing.

Jo Bevis

 Nearly all cake batters can be baked in individual portions. Bake in muffin, madeleine or ladyfinger molds.

ALMOND JOY CAKE

    1 box chocolate cake mix
    1 cup evaporated milk
    1 cup sugar
    24 large marshmallows
    1 (14 ounce) bag of coconut
1 ½ cups sugar
    ½ cup evaporated milk
    1 stick margarine
    1 (12 ounce) package chocolate chips
    1 cup toasted almonds

Bake cake mix according to package directions in a 9x13 inch or larger pan. Bring 1 cup evaporated milk and 1 cup sugar to a boil; cook 45 seconds to 1 minute. Remove from heat and add marshmallows; stir until dissolved. Add coconut and mix well. Spread on cake immediately when removed from oven. Mix remaining 1 ½ cups sugar and ½ cup evaporated milk with margarine. Bring to a boil for 15-20 seconds. Remove from heat and add chocolate chips. Melt and blend mixture. Spread over coconut mixture while cake is still warm. Sprinkle almonds on top and serve.

Sally Frierson

When baking cakes, use shiny metal pans or pans with a non-stick finish. Avoid dull, dark or enamel pans, which can cause uneven and excessive browning.

DUMP CAKE

    1 stick butter, softened
    1 large can crushed pineapple in juice
    1 can apple pie filling
    ½ cup brown sugar
    2 teaspoons cinnamon
    1 box yellow cake mix
    ½ stick butter
    1 cup chopped pecans

Mix 1 stick butter, pineapple, apple pie filling, brown sugar and cinnamon in a casserole dish. Sprinkle cake mix on top. DO NOT BLEND. Sprinkle pecans on top and dot with ½ stick butter. Bake in a 325° oven for 30 minutes or until brown on top.

Note: This cake can also be made with strawberry or cherry pie filling. Leave out the brown sugar and cinnamon for pie fillings other than apple.

Patti Sanzone

To prevent icings from becoming granular, add a pinch of salt to the sugar.

KALUHA CAKE

CAKE
- 1 box chocolate fudge cake mix without pudding
- 1 small box instant vanilla pudding
- 1 pint sour cream
- 4 eggs
- ⅓ cup Kaluha
- 1 small package chocolate chips
- ¾ cup oil

FROSTING
- 1 cup sifted powdered sugar
- ½ tablespoon cocoa
- ¼ cup Kaluha
- 1 teaspoon milk

Stir all ingredients for cake together, do not beat. Bake in a 350° oven for 45-50 minutes. To prepare frosting, mix all ingredients together. Cool cake 10-15 minutes before frosting. Garnish with mint leaves, fresh strawberries or mini chocolate chips.

Hints:
- to thicken, add powdered sugar
- to thin, add milk
- to make more chocolaty, add cocoa
- to spice up, add more Kaluha
- for almond flavor, add amaretto

Note: Any other liqueur can be substituted for the coffee liqueur.

Marcy Irwin

ITALIAN CREAM CAKE

CAKE
- 1 stick butter, softened
- ½ cup vegetable shortening
- 2 cups sugar
- 5 egg yolks
- 5 eggs whites, beaten stiff
- 1 cup chopped pecans
- 2 cups cake flour
- 1 teaspoon baking soda
- 1 cup buttermilk
- 1 teaspoon vanilla
- 1 small can coconut

FROSTING
- 1 (8 ounce) package cream cheese, softened
- 1 box powdered sugar
- 1 teaspoon vanilla
- ½ stick butter, softened
- 1 cup chopped pecans

To prepare cake, cream butter and shortening. Add sugar and beat until mixture is smooth. Add egg yolks and beat well. Combine cake flour and baking soda; add to creamed mixture, alternating with buttermilk. Stir in vanilla, pecans and coconut. Fold in beaten egg whites. Pour into 3 greased and floured 8 inch cake pans. Bake in a 350° oven for 25 minutes. Let cool completely. For frosting beat cream cheese and butter together until smooth. Add sifted powdered sugar and mix well. Add vanilla and mix again. Frost each layer and sprinkle with pecans; stack layers and frost sides.

Laura Oxendine

GOOD CAKE

   1   box yellow cake mix with pudding
   3   eggs
   1   (8 ounce) package cream cheese
   1   box confectioners sugar
   1   stick margarine

Beat 1 egg, margarine and cake mix. Pour into lightly greased 9x13 inch pan. Beat 2 eggs, cream cheese and confectioners sugar. Pour on top. Bake in a 325° oven for 40-45 minutes.

Note: ½-1 teaspoon flavoring, such as almond or cherry, may be added if desired. May also top with fruit or whipped topping.

Ann S. Lumsden

STRAWBERRY CAKE

   1   package yellow cake mix (optional white)
   1   (3 ounce) package strawberry gelatin
   ¾   cup cooking oil
   1   cup chopped nuts
   4   eggs
   2   tablespoons flour
   1   (10 ounce) package frozen strawberries

Mix all ingredients, pour into a greased, floured bundt pan and bake in a 350 oven for 45 minutes - 1 hour . Serve with whipped cream or powdered sugar.

Variation: Instead of frozen strawberries, 1 pint of fresh strawberries and ½ cup of sugar may be used.

Theresa Gagnon

DELICATE CELEBRATION CAKE

CAKE
2 ⅔ cups all-purpose flour
1 ⅞ cups sugar
4 ½ teaspoons baking powder
1 teaspoon salt
⅔ cup shortening (do not use butter or margarine)
1 ¼ cups milk
2 teaspoons vanilla
5 egg whites

FROSTING
6 tablespoons margarine or butter
1 box confectioners sugar
2 tablespoons skim milk
1 ½ tablespoons vanilla
3 squares unsweetened chocolate

Sift together flour, sugar, baking powder and salt. Add shortening. Mix milk and vanilla separately. Combine half of milk with flour mixture and beat for 2 minutes. Add remainder of milk and unbeaten egg whites. Beat for 2 minutes. Pour into 2 greased and floured 9 inch cake pans. Bake in a 350° oven for 30-35 minutes. Let cool.

For frosting: Cream butter and ½ of box of sugar. Beat in milk and vanilla. Add remaining sugar. When cool, frost and stack layers of cake. Melt chocolate and drizzle on top.

Terry Carley

BERRY MERINGUES

3   egg whites at room temperature
⅛   teaspoon cream of tartar
1   cup sugar
½   teaspoon vanilla
1   teaspoon vinegar

Grease 2 baking sheets. Beat egg whites with electric mixer until foamy. Add cream of tartar, beat until stiff. Continue beating and slowly add sugar, vanilla and vinegar. Beat until shiny, about 5 minutes. Using a ⅓ cup measuring cup as a scoop, divide meringue evenly on large baking sheets. With a rubber spatula, spread meringue into circles about 4 inches in diameter and ½ inch high. Bake at 275° for 25-30 minutes or until light brown. Cool completely

To serve, place a meringue on a dessert plate, cover with whipped cream, yogurt or ice cream. Add a scoop of raspberries, blueberries or strawberries, then cover with another meringue. Add another layer of cream/yogurt and then more berries.

Julia Spitz

When using cream of tartar, be sure to mix the batter quickly and have the oven preheated. Avoid using cream of tartar for doughs and batters that are to be stored in the refrigerator or frozen before baking.

MERINGUE TORTE

6	egg whites at room temperature
¼	teaspoon salt
½	teaspoon cream of tartar
1 ½	cups sugar
1	teaspoon vanilla extract
¼	cup light rum
1	cup heavy cream, whipped
	whole strawberries (fresh or frozen)
	canned pineapple slices, drained

Lightly butter bottom (not sides) of 9 inch tube pan. Preheat oven to 450°. In a large bowl, beat egg whites, salt and cream of tartar with an electric mixer until frothy. At high speed, beat in sugar, 2 tablespoons at a time, beating well after each addition. Add vanilla and beat until stiff peaks form when beaters are slowly raised. Turn into tube pan, spreading evenly. Place on middle rack of oven and immediately turn off heat. Let stand in oven several hours or overnight. Loosen edges with a spatula. Turn out torte on serving plate. Sprinkle surface with rum. Refrigerate until well chilled (at least 4 hours).

To serve, frost top and sides with whipped cream. Decorate top with sliced strawberries, garnish with fruit.

Note: Torte can be made the day before serving.

Ann Lumsden/Jan James   *10 servings*

CHOCOLATE KAHLUA HEAVEN

    1   box chocolate cake mix
    1   cup Kahlua
    4   boxes chocolate mousse instant pudding
    4   chocolate candy bars, frozen
    2   medium size tubs of frozen whipped topping, thawed

Prepare cake mix, following directions on box; bake in a 9x13 inch pan. Let cool. Pierce with a fork and drizzle the Kahlua over it. Chill overnight.

Break up the cake and place half in a 3 ½ quart bowl. Prepare mousse according to directions. Pour half of the mousse over the cake. Crumble 2 frozen candy bars onto the top of the mousse. Cover with 1 tub of frozen whipped topping. Repeat the process, saving some of the candy to use as a garnish.

12 servings

WILLIAMS TRIFFLE

    1   angel food cake or pound cake
    2   large packages instant vanilla pudding mix
    1   large can peaches
    1   large can strawberries
    1   large can blueberries
    1   small container frozen whipped topping

Make pudding mix according to package directions. In a large glass bowl, layer slices of cake, fruit and then vanilla pudding. Continue layering to top of bowl. Top with frozen whipped topping. Chill for at least 1 hour before serving.

Jackie Williams

GREAT-GRANDMA'S FUDGE SAUCE
(original recipe from Germany)

  1 scant cup sugar (little over ¾ cup)
  3 heaping tablespoons cocoa
  1 full cup (just a little over 1 cup) milk (homogenized, not canned)
  1 heaping tablespoon margarine or butter
  ¼ teaspoon vanilla

Mix sugar and cocoa in a saucepan, gradually add milk and then margarine or butter. Bring to a rolling boil, stirring occasionally. Boil about 10 minutes or to desired consistency. (Check consistency by putting a few drops of fudge sauce into a small amount of cool water.) Turn off heat and add vanilla. Stir, cool and pour into serving container.

Kim Cooper

OLD FASHIONED HOMEMADE FUDGE

  3 cups sugar
  ⅔ cup cocoa
  ⅛ teaspoon salt
1 ½ cups milk
  ¼ cup butter
  1 teaspoon vanilla

Butter 8 or 9 inch square pan; set aside. In a heavy 4 quart saucepan combine sugar, cocoa and salt; stir in milk. Cook over medium heat, stirring constantly until mixture comes to a full rolling boil. Boil without stirring to 234° (soft ball stage) or until syrup. If using candy thermometer, bulb should not rest on bottom of pan. Remove from heat. Add butter and vanilla. Do not stir. Cool at room temperature to 110 (luke warm). Beat with wooden spoon until fudge thickens and loses some of its gloss. Quickly spread into prepared pan and cool.

Laura Oxendine   *about 3 dozen candies*

BUTTER NUT CRUNCHIES

1	cup sugar
½	cup butter
¼	cup water
½	teaspoon salt
1 ½	cups walnuts or pecans, finely chopped and divided
1	(12 ounce) package semisweet chocolate morsels

Combine sugar, butter, water and salt in a heavy two quart saucepan; mix well. Bring to a boil; cook, stirring occasionally, until mixture reaches soft crack stage (285°). Stir in ½ cup nuts. Pour mixture into buttered 15x10x1 inch jelly roll pan, spreading to ¼ inch thickness. Let cool.

Melt chocolate over low heat; stir constantly. Spread half of chocolate over cooled candy mixture. Sprinkle with ½ cup nuts. Press nuts into chocolate and cool until firm. Invert candy and repeat process with remaining chocolate and nuts. Let cool and break into pieces. Store in airtight container.

Donna Peacock   *1 pound*

Sugar readily absorbs moisture so most candies are best stored in a cool place in tightly covered containers.

PECAN BRITTLE

    1   cup sugar
    ½   cup light corn syrup
    ¼   cup water
    ¼   teaspoon salt
    1   cup coarsely chopped pecans
    1   tablespoon butter
    1   teaspoon baking soda

Combine first four ingredients in a heavy two quart saucepan. Mix well. Cook over medium heat, stirring constantly, until mixture boils and sugar dissolves. Add pecans; return to a boil and cook, stirring frequently, until mixture reaches hard crack stage (300°). Remove from heat; immediately stir in butter and baking soda. Quickly spread mixture thinly into a buttered 15x10x1 inch jelly roll pan. Let cool; break into pieces.

Donna Peacock   *1 pound*

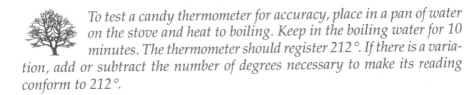 *To test a candy thermometer for accuracy, place in a pan of water on the stove and heat to boiling. Keep in the boiling water for 10 minutes. The thermometer should register 212°. If there is a variation, add or subtract the number of degrees necessary to make its reading conform to 212°.*

PEANUT BUTTER BALLS

  1 pound butter, softened
  1 pound peanut butter
  1 pound confectioners sugar
  1 (12 ounce) package chocolate chips
 ⅔ bar paraffin wax

Mix first 3 ingredients together. Roll into 1 inch or 2 inch balls. Melt chocolate and paraffin wax in a double boiler. Using a toothpick, dip balls in chocolate and place on wax paper. Refrigerate to cool.

Jennifer Craig   *approximately 180 peanut butter balls*

MAPLE PRALINES

  2 cups confectioners sugar
  1 cup maple sugar or maple syrup
 ½ cup heavy cream
  2 cups large pieces of pecans

Combine the confectioners sugar, maple sugar or maple syrup and heavy cream in a 3 quart heavy saucepan, stirring to blend well. Bring to a boil over medium heat, stirring constantly until the sugar dissolves. Cover and let boil for 2-3 minutes, then uncover and wash down the outside of the pot with a pastry brush dipped in cold water. Without stirring, boil to soft ball stage (234°). Remove from heat and let stand without stirring, until luke warm (110°). Beat with a wooden spoon until mixture starts to thicken and becomes cloudy, then beat in the pecans. Using two metal tablespoons, scoop up the mixture and drop small patties onto a sheet of wax paper. Let stand until firm, then store in an airtight container.

1 pound

TOFFEE

   2   cups firmly packed dark brown sugar
  ¼   cup butter
   1   tablespoon vinegar
       pinch of salt
   2   tablespoons boiling water

Grease a jelly roll pan or an 8x8 inch pan. Combine all the ingredients with 2 tablespoons boiling water in a 3 quart heavy saucepan, stirring well to blend. Place over moderate heat, stirring as the sugar dissolves and the mixture comes to a boil. Cover and let boil for 2-3 minutes, then uncover and wash down the outside of the pot with a pastry brush dipped in cold water. Boil slowly over moderate heat until mixture reaches hard crack stage (290°), stirring gently (without touching the sides of the pot) only if it starts to scorch. Pour mixture into the prepared pan and cool partially; cut into squares. When completely cool and hard, cut or break into pieces and transfer to an airtight tin.

MICROWAVE DIVINITY

   2   cups sugar
  ⅓   cup water
  ⅓   cup light corn syrup
  ¼   teaspoon salt
   2   egg whites
   1   teaspoon vanilla or other flavoring
  ½   cup chopped pecans (if desired)

Combine sugar, water, corn syrup and salt in a 2 quart microwave safe casserole dish, covered. Microwave on HIGH until hard ball stage or when a small amount dropped in cold water forms a ball (approximately 4-6 minutes). Let cool 3-4 minutes. While mixture is cooking and cooling beat egg whites until very stiff. Pour sugar mixture in a steady stream over egg whites, beating constantly until mixture holds its shape and starts to lose its gloss. Stir in vanilla and pecans. Drop by spoonfuls onto waxed paper.

MOUND BALLS

1 pound butter
2 pounds confectioners sugar
2 pounds flaked coconut
1 can sweetened condensed milk
2 cups nuts (almonds, pecans or walnuts)
2 teaspoons vanilla

CHOCOLATE COATING
1 (12 ounce) package semi-sweet chocolate chips
4 ounces unsweetened baking chocolate squares
3-4 tablespoons paraffin wax
round toothpicks
styrofoam sheets

In a mixing bowl, cream together butter and sugar. Add coconut, milk, nuts and vanilla; stir until blended. Chill until slightly firm; roll into balls. Insert toothpick in each ball. Place ball on cookie sheet; freeze. In a double boiler over simmering water, melt chocolate chips, chocolate squares and paraffin wax. Keep warm over hot water in double boiler. Using toothpicks as handles, dip frozen balls into chocolate mixture; stick toothpicks upright into a waxed paper-covered Styrofoam sheet. Chill until firm. Remove picks and package candy in individual paper liners. Can be placed in decorative tin. Keep refrigerated until ready to serve.

7 dozen

MILLIONAIRES

    1   pound caramels
2 ½ tablespoons milk
    2   cups pecans
    1   (12 ounce) package milk chocolate pieces
   ½ block paraffin wax

Melt caramels and milk in a double boiler. Remove from heat and beat 2-3 minutes with spoon until creamy. Add pecans. Drop by spoonfuls on buttered waxed paper. Let cool. Melt chocolate chips and paraffin in a double boiler. Using toothpicks, dip caramel nut pieces in chocolate and place back on waxed paper.

MARTHA WASHINGTON CANDY

  ½ stick butter
   1 pound confectioners sugar
   1 can sweetened condensed milk
   4 cups finely chopped pecans
   2 teaspoons vanilla or other flavoring

CHOCOLATE GLAZE
  ½ pound chocolate chips
   1 block paraffin wax

Cream butter and add sugar gradually. Add milk, vanilla and nuts. Form into balls, place on a cookie sheet and refrigerate overnight. Melt chocolate chips and paraffin in a double boiler or over low heat. Using toothpicks, dip balls into chocolate glaze until well coated. Place on waxed paper until set. Refrigerate until ready to serve.

AMARETTO TRUFFLES

    8 ounces semisweet chocolate, melted
    ¼ cup Amaretto liqueur
    2 tablespoons strong brewed coffee
    ½ cup unsalted butter, softened
    1 tablespoon vanilla
    ¾ cup vanilla wafer crumbs
    ½ cup powdered sugar
    ½ cup cocoa

In a small bowl, mix melted chocolate, Amaretto and coffee until smooth. Add butter, vanilla and cookie crumbs. Mix well. Set bowl in ice water and beat until firm. Form into balls and chill. Mix powdered sugar and cocoa. Roll truffles in the sugar mixture and store in an airtight container. Refrigerate until ready to serve.

*Note:*The truffles can also be dipped in melted chocolate instead of the powdered mixture.

 Choose crisp dry weather for dipping. Work in a room where the temperature is 60-70° and where there are no drafts.

CANDY BAR COOKIES

¾ cup butter, softened slightly
¾ cup powdered sugar
2 tablespoons evaporated milk
1 teaspoon vanilla
¼ teaspoon salt
2 cups flour

Preheat oven to 325°. Cream butter. Gradually add sifted powdered sugar. Add evaporated milk, vanilla and salt. Blend in flour. Roll out dough and cut into approximately 2x2 inch squares. Bake for 12-16 minutes or until golden brown.

CARAMEL TOPPING

½ pound (28) caramels
¼ cup evaporated milk
¼ cup butter
1 cup powdered sugar
1 cup chopped pecans

Melt caramels with evaporated milk in microwave or double boiler. Blend in butter, powdered sugar and chopped pecans. Drop a table-spoonful onto each cookie.

CHOCOLATE TOPPING

1 cup semi-sweet chocolate chips
⅓ cup evaporated milk
2 tablespoons butter
1 teaspoon vanilla
½ cup powdered sugar
24-36 pecan halves

Melt semi-sweet chocolate chips with evaporated milk. Stir butter, vanilla and powdered sugar. Drizzle over caramel and top with pe-can halves.

Carol Lanfri   *2 to 3 dozen cookies*

CRUNCHY JUMBLE COOKIES

      1   stick margarine (room temperature)
      1   cup sugar
      1   egg
      1   teaspoon vanilla
  1 ¼   cups all-purpose flour
      ½   teaspoon baking soda
      ¼   teaspoon salt
      2   cups crispy rice cereal
      1   cup chocolate chips

Cream together margarine and sugar. Beat in egg and vanilla. Mix in flour, salt and baking soda. Stir in crispy rice cereal and chocolate chips. Drop rounded tablespoonfuls of dough onto cookie sheet. Bake in a 350° oven for 12-14 minutes.

Christina S. Bischoff

NO-BAKE COOKIES

      2   cups sugar
      3   tablespoons cocoa
      ¼   cup margarine or butter
      ½   cup milk
      ½   cup peanut butter
      3   cups oats
      1   teaspoon vanilla
      ½   cup chopped nuts (optional)

In a saucepan, mix together sugar, cocoa, margarine and milk. Bring to a boil, stirring constantly. Boil for 1 minute. Remove from heat and add peanut butter; mix until melted. Add oats, vanilla and nuts, mixing well. Drop by spoonfuls onto wax paper.

Pat Thomas

CHILDHOOD THUMBPRINT COOKIES

 1   cup butter or margarine, softened
⅔   cup sugar
 2   egg yolks
 1   teaspoon vanilla
2 ¼   cups all-purpose flour
 ½   teaspoon salt

Preheat oven to 300°. Cream butter; gradually add sugar, beating until light and fluffy. Add egg yolks, one at a time, beating well after each addition. Stir in vanilla. Combine flour and salt; add to creamed mixture, mixing well. Chill mixture. Roll dough into 1 inch balls; place about 2 inches apart on ungreased cookie sheets. Press thumbprint in each cookie, leaving an indentation. Bake for 20-25 minutes; do not brown. Cool on wire racks. Place about ½ teaspoonful of chocolate frosting in each cookie indentation.

CHOCOLATE FROSTING

 1   cup sugar
 ¼   cup cocoa
 ¼   cup milk
 ¼   cup butter or margarine
 ½   teaspoon vanilla

Combine sugar, cocoa and milk in a heavy saucepan. Bring to a boil and continue boiling for 1 ½-2 minutes, stirring constantly. Remove from heat; stir in butter and vanilla. Beat until mixture is of spreading consistency. Yield: 1 cup

Jennifer Craig   *3 ½ dozen cookies*

GUM DROP COOKIES

   ¾ cup light brown sugar
   ½ cup shortening
   2 eggs
   1 teaspoon vanilla
1 ½ cups flaked coconut
   ½ cup milk
   2 cups self-rising flour
   1 cup small gum drops (more if desired)

Cream together sugar and shortening, beating until light and fluffy. Stir in eggs and vanilla; beat well. Blend in coconut and milk. Add flour all at once, stirring just to blend. Stir in gumdrops (you may slice gum drops in half, if desired). Drop by rounded teaspoonfuls onto greased cookie sheet, spacing 2 inches apart. Bake in a 350° oven for 12-15 minutes or until lightly browned. Cool on wire rack.

Shari Cromar   *5 dozen cookies*

PETTICOAT TAILS

   1 cup butter
   1 cup confectioners' sugar
   1 teaspoon vanilla
2 ½ cups flour
   1 teaspoon salt

Preheat oven to 350°. Cream butter, sugar and vanilla together. Sift together flour and salt; stir into butter mixture. Divide dough in half and roll each in wax paper. Refrigerate for 2 hours. Slice into ¼ inch pieces. Bake on ungreased cookie sheet for 8-10 minutes or until just brown around the edges.

Candy Mitchell   *3 dozen cookies*

PEANUT BUTTER TEMPTATIONS

½ cup butter or margarine
½ cup peanut butter
½ cup sugar
½ cup brown sugar
 1 egg
½ teaspoon vanilla extract
1 ¼ cups sifted flour
¾ teaspoon baking soda
½ teaspoon salt
 2 (14 ounce) bags miniature peanut butter cups (unwrap
       peanut butter cups before placing cookies in oven)

Cream butter, peanut butter and sugars together. Beat in egg and vanilla. Sift flour, baking soda and salt together. Blend into creamed mixture to make a dough. Shape dough into 1 inch balls and place into ungreased 1 ½ inch muffin tins. Bake for 8-10 minutes, or until lightly browned. Immediately after removing cookies from the oven, press a miniature peanut butter cup into the center of each cookie until only the top of the peanut butter cup shows. Let cool for 10 minutes, then remove from muffin tins. Store in airtight containers.

Note: May use large muffin tins by lining them with midget paper baking cups.

Lisa Cox   *100 cookies*

MELTING MOMENT COOKIES

    1 cup cornstarch
    1 cup confectioners' sugar
    2 cups sifted all-purpose flour
    2 cups butter or margarine (1 pound), softened
    1 teaspoon vanilla

Sift together cornstarch, sugar and flour into a bowl. Blend butter and vanilla into dry ingredients with spoon until a soft ball is formed. Shape into balls about 1 inch in diameter. Place on an ungreased cookie sheet about 1 ½ inch apart. Flatten cookies with a fork dipped in flour. Bake in a 300° oven for 15-20 minutes or until edges are lightly browned.

To further enhance the cookies:
    Add nuts or coconut; or
    Add 1 melted chocolate square or cocoa.

Note: If dough is too soft to handle, cover and chill for about 1 hour.

Robert D. Owen   *4 to 5 dozen cookies*

SAND TARTS

      1 cup butter
      ½ cup confectioners' sugar
  2 ¼ cups sifted flour
      ½ teaspoon salt
      ¼ cup chopped nuts
      1 teaspoon vanilla

Cream butter and confectioners sugar. Stir in flour and salt; mix thoroughly. Add vanilla and nuts, mixing thoroughly. Roll dough into balls and place on baking sheet. Bake in a 325° oven until light brown, approximately 20-25 minutes. Roll in confectioners' sugar after cooling.

Patti Sanzone

SCOTCH-A-ROOS

10 cups crispy rice cereal
1 cup sugar
1 cup light corn syrup
1 cup peanut butter
1 cup chocolate chips
1 cup butterscotch chips

Combine sugar and syrup in a saucepan over medium heat until melted and clear. Remove from stove. Mix in peanut butter and blend thoroughly. In a large bowl, stir mixture into crispy rice cereal. Press into bottom of a 9x13 inch pan. Melt chocolate and butterscotch chips in double boiler. Pour melted chips over crispy rice cereal mixture, spreading evenly. Cool before cutting.

Hint: Chips may be melted in microwave.

Brunetta S. Pfaender

This is an easy recipe for the young chef in the household. Flavors can be varied to meet individual tastes by using other ingredients such as nuts, coconut, or raisins.

APPLE WALNUT SQUARES

2 cups all-purpose flour
2 cups firmly packed brown sugar
1 stick butter (room temperature)
1 cup chopped walnuts
1 teaspoon cinnamon
1 teaspoon baking soda
¼ teaspoon salt
1 egg
1 cup sour cream
1 teaspoon vanilla
2 cups finely chopped tart apples (2 large apples)

Preheat oven to 350°. Lightly grease 9x13 inch pan. Combine first three ingredients in a bowl and mix until crumbled. Stir in nuts. Press 2 cups of mixture evenly into bottom of pan. Add cinnamon, baking soda and salt to remaining mixture and blend well. Beat in egg, sour cream and vanilla. Gently stir in apples. Lightly pour over mixture in pan. Bake until batter pulls away from sides of pan, about 30-40 minutes. Cool. Cut into squares.

Beulah McGlon   *24 bars*

Apples keep longer if they do not touch one another.

APRICOT ALMOND BARS

¾ cup butter
1 egg, separated
¾ cup sugar
1 teaspoon almond flavoring
½ cup (4 ounce) almond paste
2 cups flour
4 ounces of apricot jam
 sliced almonds

Beat butter, egg yolk, sugar and almond flavoring together for 5 minutes. Beat in almond paste. Mix in 2 cups flour. Press by hand into an 8x8 inch pan. Beat egg white until stiff but not dry and brush over dough. Warm apricot jam and spread over egg white. Sprinkle sliced almonds over on top of jam. Bake for 30 minutes in a 350° oven.

Note: Almond paste usually comes in a seven ounce package. Recipe can be doubled and placed in a 9x13 inch pan and baked a little longer so filling is set (approximately one hour). 1 jar of jam covers a double batch.

Patti Sanzone

 Egg whites will not beat satisfactorily if the least bit of yolk is present. Also, make sure the egg beater is free of oil.

BUTTER PECAN TURTLE BARS

2	cups all-purpose flour
¾	cup packed light brown sugar
½	cup butter, softened
1 ½	cups pecan halves
½	cup packed light brown sugar
⅔	cup butter
1 ½	cups milk chocolate chips

Combine flour, ¾ cup brown sugar and ½ cup butter. Blend until crumbly. Pat firmly onto bottom of an ungreased 9x13 inch pan. Sprinkle pecan halves over unbaked crust. Set aside.

In a small saucepan, combine ½ cup brown sugar and ⅔ cup butter. Cook over medium heat, stirring constantly, until mixture begins to boil. Boil for one minute, stirring constantly. Drizzle caramel mixture over pecans and crust. Bake in a 350° oven for 18-20 minutes or until caramel layer is bubbly and crust is lightly brown. Remove from oven and immediately sprinkle with chocolate chips. Spread chips evenly. Cool completely before cutting.

To prolong freshness of bar cookies, wrap individually in foil after cooking and cutting. They are then ready for serving, freezing or packing in lunch boxes.

POPPIN FRESH BARS

1 ¼   cups all-purpose flour
  1   cup firmly packed brown sugar
  ½   teaspoon baking soda
  ½   teaspoon salt
  ½   cup margarine or butter, softened
  1   teaspoon vanilla
  1   egg
  1   cup quick cooking oats
  1   cup semi-sweet chocolate chips
  ¼   cup chopped nuts or sunflower seeds

Optional Ingredients:
Stir one of the following into dough if desired:
  ½   cup peanut butter
  ½   cup wheat germ
  ½   cup flaked coconut
  ½   cup nonfat dry milk

Lightly spoon flour into measuring cup; level off. In a large bowl, combine all ingredients except oats, chips and nuts. Beat at medium speed until well blended. Stir in oats by hand. Add optional ingredient, if desired. Press or spread dough into bottom of greased 9x13 inch pan. Sprinkle dough with chocolate chips and nuts. Press lightly into dough. Bake in a 375° oven for 15-20 minutes or until edges are golden brown (center will be soft). Cool; loosen edges with spatula. Cut into bars.

Note: If using self-rising flour, omit baking soda and salt.

Nancy Verhine   *24 bars*

CHESS SQUARES

CRUST

   1   box yellow cake mix
   1   stick butter/margarine
   1   egg

TOPPING

   3   eggs
   1   box powdered sugar
   1   teaspoon vanilla
   1   (8 ounce) package cream cheese

Mix cake mix, butter and egg. Press into bottom of 11x13 inch glass baking dish. Mix remaining ingredients together well and pour over crust. Bake in a 350° oven for 40 minutes. Cut into squares when cool.

Note: For a variation sprinkle a handful of chocolate chips between the layers.

DIXIE BARS

  ½   pound margarine, melted
   1   cup dark brown sugar
   1   cup 10 X powdered sugar
   2   eggs
   2   cups sifted flour
  ½   teaspoon salt
   1   cup pecans, chopped
   1   teaspoon vanilla

Mix margarine with the 2 sugars. Beat in eggs, one at a time. Sift together flour and salt. Add to mixture. Add pecans and vanilla, stir well. Grease 9x11 inch or 11x13 inch pan. Pour in mixture. Bake 30 minutes in a 325° oven. While hot, cut into squares and roll in extra powdered sugar.

Pat Thomas

CHOCOLATE PIE

FILLING

1	baked 9 inch pie shell
1 ½	cups milk
1	cup sugar
	pinch of salt
3	tablespoons cocoa
3 ½	tablespoons flour
3	egg yolks, beaten
2	tablespoons butter
1	teaspoon vanilla

Cook milk, sugar, salt, cocoa and flour in the top of a double boiler. Cook (stirring constantly) until thick. Stir in egg yolks and cook a few more minutes. Remove from heat and mix in butter and vanilla. Pour into baked pie shell.

TOPPING

3	egg whites
¼	teaspoon cream of tartar
3	tablespoons sugar
½	teaspoon vanilla

Beat egg whites until frothy. Add cream of tartar and beat until stiff. Gradually add sugar and continue beating until stiff, then add vanilla. Spread over chocolate being sure to "seal" the meringue to the edge of the pie crust. Bake in a 350° oven until lightly brown - approximately 15 minutes.

Great-Grandmother Carmack

CHOCOLATE ALMOND PIE

CRUST

  2 cups pecans, finely chopped
  ½ cup sugar
  3 tablespoons butter

Combine all of the ingredients and press into a 9 inch pie pan. Bake in a 350° oven for 10 minutes and then chill for 20 minutes.

FILLING

  ½ cup milk
  6 (1 ¼ ounce) chocolate candy bars
 18 large marshmallows
  ½ teaspoon almond extract
  1 cup whipping cream

Combine milk, chocolate candy bars, marshmallows and almond extract. Cook in a double boiler until melted, stirring occasionally. Let cool. Beat whipping cream and fold into mixture. Pour into pie crust. Chill overnight.

TOPPING

  1 pint whipping cream
  1 tablespoon sugar

Beat whipping cream and sugar together and mound on top of chilled pie.

Candy Mitchell

GERMAN SWEET CHOCOLATE PIE

  1   (4 ounce) package German sweet chocolate
  ⅓ cup milk
  2   tablespoons sugar
  1   (3 ounce) package cream cheese, softened
  1   (8 ounce) container whipped topping, thawed
  1   (8 inch) graham cracker pie crust

Heat chocolate and 2 tablespoons of the milk in a saucepan over low heat. Stir until chocolate is melted. In a mixing bowl, beat sugar into cream cheese. Add the remaining milk and the melted chocolate to the mixture and beat until smooth. Fold in the whipped topping and blend until smooth. Pour into pie crust and freeze until firm, about 4 hours. Garnish with chocolate curls or extra whipped topping.

Candi Aubin

SUGARLESS APPLE PIE

  1   quart sliced apples
  ¾ cup apple juice concentrate
  2   tablespoons honey
  1   tablespoon lemon juice
  2   tablespoons cornstarch
      cinnamon to taste
  2   unbaked pie shells

Place sliced apples in an unbaked pie shell. Mix apple juice concentrate, honey and lemon juice in a saucepan. Bring to a boil. Add cornstarch that has been made into a paste with very little water. Pour over the apples. Sprinkle with cinnamon. Place remaining shell over apples and pinch edges together. Bake in a 450° oven for 15 minutes. Reduce heat to 350° and bake for 35 more minutes.

Variation: Pour above mixture over blueberries or other fresh or frozen fruit and bake as directed above.

Lila Eubanks

APPLE PIE

          2 frozen deep dish pie shells
        5-6 large granny smith apples
          1 tablespoon lemon juice
          1 tablespoon water
         ⅔ cup of sugar
         ⅛ teaspoon salt
          2 tablespoons flour
     ¼-½ teaspoon cinnamon
         ⅛ teaspoon nutmeg

Thaw pie shells. Cut up apples and pour lemon juice with water over them. Mix together sugar, salt, flour, cinnamon and nutmeg. Mix together apples and sugar mixture and put into one pie shell. Dot the apples with a small amount of margarine. Put other pie shell on top and flute edges together. Bake in a 350° oven for about 45 minutes.

Bret Dameron

TIPS FOR APPLE PIES

 When apple pie is two-thirds done, sprinkle grated cheese over the top and return to oven to finish baking.

 To make your apple pie look crunchy, blend together 1 tablespoon of shortening, 1 tablespoon of sugar, 3 tablespoons of flour and ¼ teaspoon salt. Brush unbaked pie with milk, then sprinkle this mixture on top.

MANDARIN ORANGE YOGURT PIE

2   small containers mandarin orange yogurt
1   small can mandarin oranges, drained
1   small container frozen whipped topping, thawed
1   prepared graham cracker pie crust

Mix all the ingredients together and pour into the graham cracker crust. Freeze for several hours before serving. Different flavors of yogurt and types of fruit can be substituted as desired.

Terri Pate

CHERRY MUM MUM PIE

CRUST
2   cups plain flour
2   sticks margarine (do not melt, set out and let soften)
1   cup chopped pecans

Mix until crumbly and pat into an 11x13 inch baking dish. Bake in a 350° oven for 30 minutes . Cool completely.

FILLING
1   (8 ounce) package cream cheese
1   box powdered sugar
1   (12 ounce) container whipped topping, thawed
2   teaspoons lemon juice
2   cans cherry pie filling

Mix cream cheese, sugar, whipped topping and lemon juice with a mixer until well blended. Spoon over cooked crust and top with cherry pie filling. Refrigerate at least 2 hours before serving.

Rae Palestro

SWEET POTATO MOLASSES PIE

3 medium sweet potatoes or 1 (17 ounce) can of yams
1 unbaked pie shell
½ cup packed brown sugar
½ cup molasses
1 teaspoon ground cinnamon
½ teaspoon ground ginger
½ teaspoon nutmeg
¼ teaspoon salt
3 eggs, slightly beaten
1 cup milk

In a medium saucepan, cover the raw sweet potatoes with salted water and cook for 20-25 minutes or until tender. Drain and cool slightly, then peel and mash the potatoes. Mix together sweet potatoes, brown sugar, molasses, cinnamon, ginger, nutmeg and salt. Add eggs and milk to sweet potato mixture, mixing well. Pour the mixture into the pie shell. Cover the crust edge with foil and bake in a 375° oven for 20 minutes. Remove foil and bake for 30-35 more minutes or until knife inserted comes out clean. Serve with whipped cream if desired.

To keep pie crust from becoming soggy is to sprinkle it with equal parts sugar and flour before adding the filling.

SENSATIONAL DOUBLE LAYER PUMPKIN PIE

4	ounces light cream cheese, softened
1	tablespoon milk
1	tablespoon sugar
1 ½	cups frozen whipped topping, thawed
1	graham cracker crust
1	cup milk
2	packages vanilla flavor instant pudding (4 serving size)
1	(16 ounce) can pumpkin
1-2	teaspoons pumpkin spice (cinnamon, ginger, clove)

Bottom Layer: Mix cream cheese, 1 tablespoon milk and sugar in a large bowl with whisk. Gently stir in thawed whipped topping. Spread on bottom of graham cracker crust.

Top Layer: Pour 1 cup milk into a mixing bowl. Add pudding mix. Beat with whisk until well blended or 1-2 minutes (mixture will be thick). Stir in pumpkin and spices and mix well with whisk. Spread pumpkin mixture over cream cheese layer. Refrigerate at least 3 hours. Garnish with whipped topping and nuts if desired.

Judy Wheaton

Crumb crusts need not be baked before filling. If used unbaked, be sure to first chill thoroughly or the filling will immediately disintegrate the crust.

Equivalent
Measures

Bellevue

Surrounded by great oaks and magnolias, Bellevue was the 500-acre plantation home of Princess Catherine Murat, the great grand-niece of George Washington and widow of Prince Achille Murat, the nephew of Napoleon Bonaparte. The home was constructed between 1838 and 1841, and purchased by the Princess in 1854. She named it "Bellevue" in memory of a hotel in Brussels where she and the Prince had spent many happy days. The Princess furnished Bellevue with opulent chairs, tables, and mirrors from the Bonapartes of Paris. The dining room was resplendent with gold plate, antique silver, crested china, and fine linen.

The Princess entertained her friends and led an active public life while residing in Tallahassee during a part of each year. She had the distinction of firing the cannon announcing Florida's secession from the Union during the War Between the States. During the war, the Princess used her own funds and sold her jewels to aid the sick and the wounded. By the time of General Lee's surrender she was so impoverished that she had to request aid from the Union headquarters in Tallahassee. Following a desperate appeal for help after the war, the Bonaparte Regime provided her with financial assistance. The Princess died in 1867.

In the 1960's, Bellevue was scheduled for demolition to make room for an apartment complex. Through community efforts, Bellevue was saved from destruction and in 1967, the house was moved from its original location to the Tallahassee Museum of History and Natural Science. The Museum plans to restore Bellevue to its original splendor. Bellevue has been entered on the National Register of Historic Places.

Equivalent Weights and Measures

Food	Weight	Measure
Apples	1 pound (3 medium)	3 cups, sliced
Bananas	1 pound (3 medium)	2 ½ cups, sliced
Bread	1 pound	12-16 slices
Butter or margarine	1 pound	2 cups
Butter or margarine	¼ pound stick	½ cup
Candied fruit or peels	½ pound	1 ¼ cups, cut
Cheese, American	1 pound	4-5 cups, shredded
Cottage cheese	1 pound	2 cups
Cream cheese	3 ounces	6 tablespoons
Cocoa	1 pound	4 cups
Coconut, flaked or shredded	1 pound	5 cups
Coffee	1 pound	80 tablespoons
Cornmeal	1 pound	3 cups
Cream, heavy	½ pint	2 cups, whipped
Dates, pitted	1 pound	2-3 cups, chopped
Dates, pitted	7 ¼ package	1 ¼ cups, chopped
Flour		
All-purpose	1 pound	4 cups, sifted
Cake	1 pound	4 ¾-5 cups, sifted
Whole Wheat	1 pound	3 ½ cups, unsifted
Lemon Juice	1 medium	2-3 tablespoons
Lemon Rind	1 medium	2 teaspoons, grated
Milk		
Evaporated	6 ounce can	¾ cup
Evaporated	14 ½ ounce can	1 ⅔ cup
Sweetened condensed	14 ounce can	1 ¼ cups
Nuts, in shell		
Almonds	1 pound	1-1 ¾ cups
Nutmeats		
Peanuts	1 pound	2 cups nutmeats
Pecans	1 pound	2 ¼ cups nutmeats
Walnuts	1 pound	1 ⅔ cup nutmeats

Food	Weight	Measure
Nuts, Shelled		
Almonds	1 pound, 2 ounces	4 cups
Peanuts	1 pound	4 cups
Pecans	1 pound	4 cups
Walnuts	1 pound	3 cups
Orange, Juice	1 medium	⅓ cup
Orange, Rind	1 medium	2 tablespoons, grated
Raisins, Seedless	1 pound	3 cups
Sugar		
Brown	1 pound	2 ¼ cups, firmly packed
Powdered	1 pound	3 ½ cups, unsifted
Granulated	1 pound	2 cups

Equivalent Chart

3 teaspoons .... 1 tablespoon
4 tablespoons .... ¼ cup
8 tablespoons .... ½ cup
16 tablespoons .... 1 cup
1 cup .... 8 fluid ounces
2 cups.. 1 pint (16 fluid ounces)
⅛ cup .... 2 tablespoons
⅓ cup .... 5 tablespoons plus 1 teaspoon
⅔ cup .... 10 tablespoons plus 2 teaspoons
¾ cup .... 12 tablespoons
1 quart .... 2 pints or 4 cups
1 pound .... 16 ounces
Few grains or dash .... Less than ⅛ teaspoon
Pinch .... As much as can be between tip of finger and thumb

Index

San Luis Archaeological and Historic Site

At San Luis Archaeological and Historic Site, a portion of Tallahassee's past is unearthed every day. Beginning in the 1630's the Spaniards, who had settled in St. Augustine in 1565, came to Spanish Florida's Apalachee Province to extend their mission system and to convert the natives to Christianity. The Spaniards took advantage of the abundant agricultural resources and labor force, and soon Mission San Luis de Talimali became the capital of the mission system in the province. The prosperous mission, which had access to imported goods such as silk and porcelain, consisted of a European-style church and friary, a round thatched-roof council house for the Apalachee large enough to hold 3,000 people, a plaza, and Spanish and Apalachee villages. The two cultures lived together successfully until British-instigated raids in 1704 caused the Spaniards to burn the fort and return to St. Augustine. Those Apalachee who survived the attacks also abandoned the area.

Today, archaeologists continue to find clues and artifacts about life at San Luis during the 1600's. Periodically, live interpreters dressed in period clothing reenact the lifestyle of the historic 17th-century mission. San Luis has been designated a National Historic Landmark.

INDEX

A

ACCOMPANIMENTS
Ambrosia, 240
Apple Scallop, 239
Cranberry Relish, 240
Cranberry-Spiced Pears, 244
Curried Fruit, 243
DRESSING
  Apricot Dressing, 231
  Bread Dressing, 232
  Celery Dressing, 232
  Cornbread Dressing, 232
  Giblet Dressing, 232
  Oyster Dressing, 232
  Paul's Turkey Dressing, 231
Fruit Compote, 241
GRAVY
  Giblet Gravy, 233
Ham Glaze, 233
Honeyed Strawberries and Bananas, 244
Hot Fruit Compote, 241
Mai Tai Compote, 242
Maple Candied Apples, 238
MARINADE
  Marinade for Domestic, Meat, Game or Fowl, 235
  Marinade for Game, 234
  Steak Marinade, 234
  Turkey Basting Marinade, 234
Roasted Sweet Peppers, 238
SAUCE
  Cocktail Sauce, 236
  Cream Sauce, 237
  Easy Barbecue Sauce, 236
  Tartar Sauce, 237
Sauerkraut Relish, 233
Scalloped Pineapple, 243
Spiced Blueberries, 239
Spiced Peaches, 242
STUFFING

Black Bean Stuffing, 229
Corn Stuffing, 230
Wild Rice Stuffing, 230
Almond Joy Cake, 255
Amaretto Truffles, 271
Ambrosia, 240
APPETIZERS
  Caviar Appetizers, 28
  Cheese Ball, 23
  Chicken Puffs, 30
  Chilled Mexican Appetizer, 27
  Chutney Roll, 26
  Deviled Ham n' Egg Salad, 29
DIP
  Aunt Joyce's Dip, 19
  Black Bean Dip, 18
  Chalupa (Layered Dip), 19
  Cheese Dip, 20
  Cheesy Garlic Artichoke Dip, 20
  Chipped Beef Dip, 23
  Clam Dip, 15
  Crab Dip, 15
  Crab Meat Con Queso Dip, 16
  Heated Mexican Dip, 18
  Hot Crab Meat Sherry Dip, 16
  Joan's Award Winning Shrimp Dip, 17
  "Skinny" Dip for Vegetables or Crackers, 21
  Spinach Dip, 22
  Tahini (Sesame Paste Dip), 17
  Vegetable Dip, 22
  Vidalia Onion Dip, 21
Easy Cheese Wafers, 24
Herbed Chicken Wings, 31
Holiday Appetizer Pie, 27
Luau Bites, 29
Penuche Nuts, 25
Pickups, 32
Seminole Crackers, 24
Spicy Meatballs, 28
Spinach Balls, 25

Spinach Pate, 33
Teriyaki Chicken Wings, 30
Tiger Catnip, 26
Toast Points, 33
Tri Stuffed Celery, 32
Apple Pie, 287
Apple Scallop, 239
Apple Walnut Squares, 279
Applesauce Fruit Cake, 253
Apricot Almond Bars, 280
Apricot Bread, 77
Apricot Chicken, 124
Apricot Dressing, 231
Apricot-Glazed Sweet Potatoes, 220
Apricot-Pineapple Salad, 57
Artichoke Hearts with Spinach, 202
Artichokes with Avgolemono Sauce, 201
Asparagus Casserole, 203
Aunt Helen Moore's Champagne
    Punch, 35
Aunt Joyce's Dip, 19

B

Baked Chops with Vegetables, 112
Baked Flounder, 159
Baked Lima Beans, 207
Baked Quail, 141
Baked Red Snapper, 164
Baked Stuffed Peppers, 135
Baked Tomatoes Stuffed with Chicken
    & Spinach, 127
Banana Bread, 78
Banana Pound Cake, 251
BEEF
    Beef and Broccoli, 102
    Brazilian Pot Roast, 103
    Cape Cod Cranberry Meatloaf, 100
    Crescent Beef Roll, 97
    Easy Ribs, 103
    Festive Fajitas, 105
    Fiesta, 106
    Hamburger Pie, 97
    Marinated Beef Tenderloin, 101
    Neapolitan Meatloaf, 99

Secret Ribs, 104
Swiss Steak, 104
Waikiki Meatballs, 98
Beef and Broccoli, 102
Berry Meringues, 261
BEVERAGES
    Coffee Frappe, 39
    Hot Cranberry Tea, 40
    Mistletoe Mull, 37
    Mulled Cider, 38
    PUNCH
        Aunt Helen Moore's Champagne
            Punch, 35
        Cranberry Punch, 36
        Fruit Punch, 37
        Mint Punch, 35
        Orange Sparkler, 36
        Party Punch, 34
        Virginia Settler's Punch, 34
    Quick Russian Tea, 40
    Rosemary Lemonade, 39
    Wassail, 38
Black Bean Burritos, 166
Black Bean Dip, 18
Black Bean Soup, 55
Black Bean Stuffing, 229
Blender Carrot Cake, 248
Blue Crab Salad, 60
Braised Doves, 146
Brazilian Pot Roast, 103
Brazilian Shrimp and Cheese Casserole,
    156
Bread Dressing, 232
BREADS
    Apricot Bread, 77
    Banana Bread, 78
    BISCUITS
        Grandmother Jesse's Riz Biscuits,
            70
        Praline Biscuits, 71
        Sour Cream Biscuits, 70
        Virginia Buttermilk Biscuits, 72
    Clam Fritters, 82
    Cranberry Fruit and Nut Bread, 79
    Date and Nut Bread, 80

Easy Cheese Bread, 81
King Arthur Popovers, 72
Monkey Bread, 75
MUFFINS
Fruity Muffins, 68
Pumpkin Muffins, 69
Refrigerator Bran Muffins, 67
Onion Cheese Supper Bread, 82
ROLLS
Grandmother Spitz's Refrigerator Rolls, 74
Parker House Rolls, 73
Sausage Rolls, 75
Strawberry Nut Bread, 80
Waffles, 67
Zucchini Bread, 76
Brie Soup, 48
Broccoli Casserole, 208
Broccoli Cheese Stuffed Shells, 173
Broccoli Soup, 51
Broccoli with Lemon Sauce, 208
Broiled Scallops, 152
Brussels Sprouts Almandine, 209
Butter Nut Crunchies, 265
Butter Pecan Turtle Bars, 281

C

Cajun Chicken Pasta, 184
CAKES
4 Banana Pound Cake, 251
Almond Joy Cake, 255
Applesauce Fruit Cake, 253
Berry Meringues, 261
Blender Carrot Cake, 248
Chocolate Kahlua Heaven, 263
Chocolate Sour Cream Pound Cake, 251
Delicate Celebration Cake, 260
Dump Cake, 256
Good Cake, 259
Harvest Pumpkin Cheesecake, 252
Hummingbird Cake, 247
Italian Cream Cake, 258
Kaluha Cake, 257

Lemonade Cake, 254
Meringue Torte, 262
Michigan Pound Cake, 250
Nannie's Cake, 249
Sour Cream Coffee Cake, 250
Strawberry Cake, 259
Williams Triffle, 263
Calico Beans, 204
CANDY
Amaretto Truffles, 271
Butter Nut Crunchies, 265
Great-Grandma's Fudge Sauce, 264
Maple Pralines, 267
Martha Washington Candy, 270
Microwave Divinity, 268
Millionaires, 270
Mound Balls, 269
Old Fashioned Homemade Fudge, 264
Peanut Butter Balls, 267
Pecan Brittle, 266
Toffee, 268
Candy Bar Cookies, 272
Cantonese Duck, 144
Cape Cod Cranberry Meatloaf, 100
Carrot Fritters, 212
Carrots Au Gratin, 212
Cauliflower Salad, 61
Caviar Appetizers, 28
Celery Dressing, 232
Chalupa (Layered Dip), 19
CHEESE
Cheese Grits With Sausage, 86
Chile Cheese Grits, 87
Easy Cheese Brunch Casserole, 85
New England Cheese Puffs, 86
Cheese Ball, 23
Cheese Dip, 20
Cheese Grits With Sausage, 86
Cheesy Garlic Artichoke Dip, 20
Cherry Mum Mum Pie, 288
Chess Squares, 283
Chicken & Dumplings, 121
Chicken and Black Bean Enchiladas, 133
Chicken and Noodles, 185

Chicken and Pasta Stew, 48
Chicken Breast Alfredo, 123
Chicken Breasts, 118
Chicken Breasts in Port, 124
Chicken Divan, 126
Chicken Enchiladas, 132
Chicken in Wine Sauce, 126
Chicken Italiano, 119
Chicken Parmigiana, 119
Chicken Pot Pie, 125
Chicken Puffs, 30
Chicken with Artichokes and Pistachio
     Nuts, 128
Chicken with Lemon Sauce, 120
Chicken with Tarragon Caper Sauce,
     122
Chicken with Tortellini, 184
Childhood Thumbprint Cookies, 274
Chile Cheese Grits, 87
Chili #1: Hot and Spicy, 45
Chili #2: Meatless Chili, 46
Chili Relleno Casserole, 165
Chilled Mexican Appetizer, 27
Chinese New Year Rice, 194
Chipped Beef Dip, 23
Chocolate Almond Pie, 285
Chocolate Kahlua Heaven, 263
Chocolate Pie, 284
Chocolate Sour Cream Pound Cake, 251
Chutney Roll, 26
Clam Dip, 15
Clam Fritters, 82
Cocktail Sauce, 236
Coffee Frappe, 39
Cold Peach Soup with Blueberries, 43
Congealed Cranberry-Sour Cream
     Salad, 58
COOKIES & BARS
  Apple Walnut Squares, 279
  Apricot Almond Bars, 280
  Butter Pecan Turtle Bars, 281
  Candy Bar Cookies, 272
  Chess Squares, 283
  Childhood Thumbprint Cookies, 274
  Crunchy Jumble Cookies, 273

  Dixie Bars, 283
  Gum Drop Cookies, 275
  Melting Moment Cookies, 277
  No-Bake Cookies, 273
  Peanut Butter Temptations, 276
  Petticoat Tails, 275
  Poppin Fresh Bars, 282
  Sand Tarts, 277
  Scotch-A-Roos, 278
Corn Casserole, 213
Corn Fritters, 213
Corn Stuffing, 230
Cornbread Dressing, 232
Cornish Hens, 146
Crab Dip, 15
Crab Imperial, 150
Crab Meat Con Queso Dip, 16
Cranberry Fruit and Nut Bread, 79
Cranberry Punch, 36
Cranberry Relish, 240
Cranberry-Spiced Pears, 244
Cream Sauce, 237
Creamed Cabbage with Walnuts, 211
Crescent Beef Roll, 97
Crispy Potato Wedges, 219
Crock Pot Chicken and Spaghetti, 185
Crunchy Jumble Cookies, 273
Curried Fruit, 243
Curried Shrimp and Rice Salad, 56

D

Delicate Celebration Cake, 260
DESSERTS
  CAKES
    4 Banana Pound Cake, 251
    Almond Joy Cake, 255
    Applesauce Fruit Cake, 253
    Berry Meringues, 261
    Blender Carrot Cake, 248
    Chocolate Kahlua Heaven, 263
    Chocolate Sour Cream Pound
       Cake, 251
    Delicate Celebration Cake, 260
    Dump Cake, 256

Good Cake, 259
Harvest Pumpkin Cheesecake, 252
Hummingbird Cake, 247
Italian Cream Cake, 258
Kaluha Cake, 257
Lemonade Cake, 254
Meringue Torte, 262
Michigan Pound Cake, 250
Nannie's Cake, 249
Sour Cream Coffee Cake, 250
Strawberry Cake, 259
Williams Triffle, 263

CANDY
Amaretto Truffles, 271
Butter Nut Crunchies, 265
Great-Grandma's Fudge Sauce, 264
Maple Pralines, 267
Martha Washington Candy, 270
Microwave Divinity, 268
Millionaires, 270
Mound Balls, 269
Old Fashioned Homemade
    Fudge, 264
Peanut Butter Balls, 267
Pecan Brittle, 266
Toffee, 268

COOKIES & BARS
Apple Walnut Squares, 279
Apricot Almond Bars, 280
Butter Pecan Turtle Bars, 281
Candy Bar Cookies, 272
Chess Squares, 283
Childhood Thumbprint Cookies,
    274
Crunchy Jumble Cookies, 273
Dixie Bars, 283
Gum Drop Cookies, 275
Melting Moment Cookies, 277
No-Bake Cookies, 273
Peanut Butter Temptations, 276
Petticoat Tails, 275
Poppin Fresh Bars, 282
Sand Tarts, 277
Scotch-A-Roos, 278

PIES
Apple Pie, 287
Cherry Mum Mum Pie, 288
Chocolate Almond Pie, 285
Chocolate Pie, 284
Fruit Pizza Pie, 290
German Sweet Chocolate Pie, 286
Key Lime Pie, 289
Mandarin Orange Yogurt Pie, 288
Pineapple Pie, 289
Sensational Double Layer
    Pumpkin Pie, 292
Sugarless Apple Pie, 286
Sweet Potato Molasses Pie, 291
Deviled Ham n' Egg Salad, 29
Deviled Tomatoes, 225
Dilled Tuna Salad, 60
Dixie Bars, 283

DRESSING
Apricot Dressing, 231
Bread Dressing, 232
Cornbread Dressing, 232
Paul's Turkey Dressing, 231
Dump Cake, 256

E

Easy Barbecue Sauce, 236
Easy Cheese Bread, 81
Easy Cheese Brunch Casserole, 85
Easy Cheese Wafers, 24
Easy Ribs, 103
Egg and Sausage Quiche, 94
Eggplant Aubergine Salad, 56

EGGS
Egg and Sausage Quiche, 94
Eggs Ponce de Leon, 88
Herb and Nut Omelet, 89
Mushroom Quiche, 91
Nancy's Spinach Quiche, 90
Seafood Quiche with Rice Crust, 93
Wild Rice and Mushroom Quiche, 92
Eggs Ponce de Leon, 88

ENTREES
  BEEF
    Beef and Broccoli, 102
    Brazilian Pot Roast, 103
    Cape Cod Cranberry Meatloaf, 100
    Crescent Beef Roll, 97
    Easy Ribs, 103
    Festive Fajitas, 105
    Fiesta, 106
    Hamburger Pie, 97
    Marinated Beef Tenderloin, 101
    Neapolitan Meatloaf, 99
    Secret Ribs, 104
    Swiss Steak, 104
    Waikiki Meatballs, 98
  GAME
    Baked Quail, 141
    Braised Doves, 146
    Cantonese Duck, 144
    Cornish Hens, 146
    Grilled Venison Loin (Backstrap), 141
    Rabbit Stew, 148
    Roast Duck with Chambord and Grand Mariner, 143
    Roast Pheasant with Brandy and Cream, 142
    Roast Wild Duck, 145
    Smoked Wild Duck, 145
    Venison Curry, 139
    Venison or Elk Stew, 140
    Venison Ragout, 137
    Venison Scallopini, 138
    Venison Steak, 136
    Wild Goose, 147
  LAMB
    Lamb Shanks in Red Wine, 107
    Lamb Stew, 108
    Spicy Leg of Lamb, 109
  PORK
    Baked Chops with Vegetables, 112
    Ham Loaf, 115
    Mazetti, 117
    Pineapple Pork Roast, 114
    Pork Chop and Potato Scallop, 111
    Pork Chops in Tomato and Pepper Sauce, 110
    Pork Chops with Apples & Bourbon, 113
    Sausage-Vegetable Dinner, 116
    Scalloped Potatoes and Ham, 116
    Spicy Pork Roast, 113
    Sweet-and-Sour Pork Chops, 111
  POULTRY
    Apricot Chicken, 124
    Baked Stuffed Peppers, 135
    Baked Tomatoes Stuffed with Chicken & Spinach, 127
    Chicken & Dumplings, 121
    Chicken and Black Bean Enchiladas, 133
    Chicken Breast Alfredo, 123
    Chicken Breasts, 118
    Chicken Breasts in Port, 124
    Chicken Divan, 126
    Chicken Enchiladas, 132
    Chicken in Wine Sauce, 126
    Chicken Italiano, 119
    Chicken Parmigiana, 119
    Chicken Pot Pie, 125
    Chicken with Artichokes and Pistachio Nuts, 128
    Chicken with Lemon Sauce, 120
    Chicken with Tarragon Caper Sauce, 122
    Foiled Chicken with Lemon and Herbs, 118
    Hungarian Chicken, 131
    Kraut Chicken, 122
    Ovenbaked Chicken Kiev, 130
    Pecan-Breaded Chicken with Mustard Sauce, 129
    So Good Leftover Turkey, 135
    Vegetable Turkey Pie, 134
  SEAFOOD
    Baked Flounder, 159
    Baked Red Snapper, 164
    Brazilian Shrimp and Cheese Casserole, 156
    Broiled Scallops, 152

Crab Imperial, 150
Florida Snapper with Green
	Peppercorn Sauce, 163
Flounder Ambassador, 160
Ginger Steamed Bass, 149
Grouper Fillets, 159
Hunter's Bluefish with
	Horseradish Sauce, 158
Marinated Tuna Steaks, 165
Overnight Salmon Strata, 162
Oyster Bake, 151
Salmon Loaf with Cucumber
	Sauce, 161
Sauteed Shrimp, 153
Seviche, 153
Shrimp Creole, 154
Shrimp Etouffee, 155
Shrimp Newburg, 150
Stacey's Low Country Boil, 157
VEGETARIAN
Black Bean Burritos, 166
Chili Relleno Casserole, 165
Fried Tofu, 169
Gardener's Pizza, 168
Italian Spaghetti and Pecan Balls,
	167
Zucchini Pie, 170

F

Festive Fajitas, 105
Fiesta, 106
Florida Snapper with Green Peppercorn
	Sauce, 163
Flounder Ambassador, 160
Foiled Chicken with Lemon and Herbs,
	118
Ford-Hook Lima Beans Plus, 206
Fried Green Pepper Rings, 217
Fried Green Tomatoes, 225
Fried Tofu, 169
Fruit Bowl, 62
Fruit Compote, 241
Fruit Pizza Pie, 290
Fruit Punch, 37

Fruit Slaw, 63
Fruity Muffins, 68

G

GAME
Baked Quail, 141
Braised Doves, 146
Cantonese Duck, 144
Cornish Hens, 146
Grilled Venison Loin (Backstrap), 141
Rabbit Stew, 148
Roast Duck with Chambord and
	Grand Mariner, 143
Roast Pheasant with Brandy and
	Cream, 142
Roast Wild Duck, 145
Smoked Wild Duck, 145
Venison Curry, 139
Venison or Elk Stew, 140
Venison Ragout, 137
Venison Scallopini, 138
Venison Steak, 136
Wild Goose, 147
Gardener's Pizza, 168
German Sweet Chocolate Pie, 286
Giblet Dressing, 232
Giblet Gravy, 233
Ginger Steamed Bass, 149
Good Cake, 259
Grandmother Jesse's Riz Biscuits, 70
Grandmother Spitz's Refrigerator Rolls,
	74
GRAVY
Giblet Gravy, 232
Great-Grandma's Fudge Sauce, 264
Green Beans India, 206
Green Beans with Herbs, 205
Grilled Tomato Sauce, 183
Grilled Venison Loin (Backstrap), 141
Grouper Fillets, 159
Gum Drop Cookies, 275

H

Ham Glaze, 233
Ham Loaf, 115
Hamburger Pie, 97
Harvest Pumpkin Cheesecake, 252
Heated Mexican Dip, 18
Herb and Nut Omelet, 89
Herbed Chicken Wings, 31
Herbed White Bean Salad, 62
Holiday Appetizer Pie, 27
Honeyed Strawberries and
    Bananas, 244
Hopping John, 194
Hot and Sour Soup, 49
Hot Crab Meat Sherry Dip, 16
Hot Cranberry Tea, 40
Hot Fruit Compote, 241
Hummingbird Cake, 247
Hungarian Chicken, 131
Hunter's Bluefish with Horseradish
    Sauce, 158

I

Ice Box Slaw, 64
Italian Cream Cake, 258
Italian Spaghetti and Pecan Balls, 167
Italian Surprise, 192

J

Joan's Award Winning Shrimp Dip, 17

K

Kaluha Cake, 257
Key Lime Pie, 289
King Arthur Popovers, 72
Kraut Chicken, 122

L

LAMB
    Lamb Shanks in Red Wine, 107
    Lamb Stew, 108
    Spicy Leg of Lamb, 109
Lamb Shanks in Red Wine, 107
Lamb Stew, 108
Layered Spinach Salad, 64
Lemon Dill Rice, 197
Lemonade Cake, 254
Lentil Soup, 54
Linguini with Red Seafood Sauce, 189
Luau Bites, 29

M

Mai Tai Compote, 242
Mandarin Orange Yogurt Pie, 288
Manicotti Cheese Bake, 176
Maple Candied Apples, 238
Maple Pralines, 267
MARINADE
    Marinade for Domestic, Meat, Game
        or Fowl, 235
    Marinade for Game, 234
    Steak Marinade, 234
    Turkey Basting Marinade, 234
Marinade for Domestic, Meat, Game or
    Fowl, 235
Marinade for Game, 234
Marinated Beef Tenderloin, 101
Marinated Tuna Steaks, 165
Martha Washington Candy, 270
Mazetti, 117
Melting Moment Cookies, 277
Meringue Torte, 262
Mexi-Bean Pasta, 178
Michigan Pound Cake, 250
Microwave Divinity, 268
Millionaires, 270
Mint Punch, 35
Mistletoe Mull, 37
Monkey Bread, 75
Mother's Cucumber Soup, 44
Mound Balls, 269
Mrs. Correli's Eggplant Casserole, 214
MUFFINS
    Fruity Muffins, 68

Pumpkin Muffins, 69
Refrigerator Bran Muffins, 67
Mulled Cider, 38
Mushroom Quiche, 91
Mushroom Strudel, 215

N

Nancy's Spinach Quiche, 90
Nannie's Cake, 249
Neapolitan Meatloaf, 99
New England Cheese Puffs, 86
No-Bake Cookies, 273

O

Old Fashion Beef Stew, 53
Old Fashioned Homemade Fudge, 264
Onion Cheese Supper Bread, 82
Orange Beets, 207
Orange Sparkler, 36
Ovenbaked Chicken Kiev, 130
Overnight Salmon Strata, 162
Oyster Bake, 151
Oyster Dressing, 232

P

Paella, 198
Paella Rice Mix, 198
Parker House Rolls, 73
Parmesan Eggplant with Yogurt, 214
Party Punch, 34
PASTA
    Broccoli Cheese Stuffed Shells, 173
    Cajun Chicken Pasta, 184
    Chicken and Noodles, 185
    Chicken with Tortellini, 184
    Crock Pot Chicken and Spaghetti, 185
    Grilled Tomato Sauce, 183
    Italian Surprise, 192
    Linguini with Red Seafood Sauce, 189
    Manicotti Cheese Bake, 176
    Mexi-Bean Pasta, 178
    Pasta with Peas, Tomatoes and Feta
        Cheese, 179

Romanof Beef Noodle Casserole, 193
Sassy Spaghetti, 182
Seafood Fettuccine, 190
Seafood Lasagna, 191
Shrimp and Scallops Pasta, 188
Sopa Seca de Fideo, 181
Spaghetti Reina, 182
Spicy Lentil Spaghetti, 177
Stuffed Shells Florentine, 175
Sun-dried Tomato Spaghetti Sauce,
    181
Tortellini with Dill Pesto, 174
Turkey Lasagna, 186
Turkey Tetrazzini, 187
Vegetable Lasagna, 180
Pasta with Peas, Tomatoes and Feta
    Cheese, 179
Paul's Turkey Dressing, 231
Peanut Butter Balls, 267
Peanut Butter Temptations, 276
Peas with Mint, 217
Pecan Brittle, 266
Pecan-Breaded Chicken with Mustard
    Sauce, 129
Penuche Nuts, 25
Petticoat Tails, 275
Piccadillo (Spanish Stew), 47
Pickups, 32
PIES
    Apple Pie, 287
    Cherry Mum Mum Pie, 288
    Chocolate Almond Pie, 285
    Chocolate Pie, 284
    Fruit Pizza Pie, 290
    German Sweet Chocolate Pie, 286
    Key Lime Pie, 289
    Mandarin Orange Yogurt Pie, 288
    Pineapple Pie, 289
    Sensational Double Layer Pumpkin
        Pie, 292
    Sugarless Apple Pie, 286
    Sweet Potato Molasses Pie, 291
Pineapple Pie, 289
Pineapple Pork Roast, 114
Poppin Fresh Bars, 282

PORK
Baked Chops with Vegetables, 112
Ham Loaf, 115
Mazetti, 117
Pineapple Pork Roast, 114
Pork Chop and Potato Scallop, 111
Pork Chops in Tomato and Pepper
   Sauce, 110
Pork Chops with Apples & Bourbon,
   113
Sausage-Vegetable Dinner, 116
Scalloped Potatoes and Ham, 116
Spicy Pork Roast, 113
Sweet-and-Sour Pork Chops, 111
Pork Chop and Potato Scallop, 111
Pork Chops in Tomato and Pepper
   Sauce, 110
Pork Chops with Apples & Bourbon,
   113
Potato Casserole, 216
Potato Soup with Rivels, 50
POULTRY
Apricot Chicken, 124
Baked Stuffed Peppers, 135
Baked Tomatoes Stuffed with
   Chicken & Spinach, 127
Chicken & Dumplings, 121
Chicken and Black Bean Enchiladas,
   133
Chicken Breast Alfredo, 123
Chicken Breasts, 118
Chicken Breasts in Port, 124
Chicken Divan, 126
Chicken Enchiladas, 132
Chicken in Wine Sauce, 126
Chicken Italiano, 119
Chicken Parmigiana, 119
Chicken Pot Pie, 125
Chicken with Artichokes and
   Pistachio Nuts, 128
Chicken with Lemon Sauce, 120
Chicken with Tarragon Caper Sauce,
   122
Foiled Chicken with Lemon and
   Herbs, 118

Hungarian Chicken, 131
Kraut Chicken, 122
Ovenbaked Chicken Kiev, 130
Pecan-Breaded Chicken with
   Mustard Sauce, 129
So Good Leftover Turkey, 135
Vegetable Turkey Pie, 134
Praline Biscuits, 71
Pumpkin Muffins, 69
Pumpkin Soup, 52
PUNCH
Aunt Helen Moore's Champagne
   Punch, 35
Cranberry Punch, 36
Fruit Punch, 37
Mint Punch, 35
Orange Sparkler, 36
Party Punch, 34
Virginia Settler's Punch, 34

Q

Quick Red Beans and Rice, 195
Quick Russian Tea, 40

R

Rabbit Stew, 148
Red Cabbage and Apples, 210
Refrigerator Bran Muffins, 67
RICE
Chinese New Year Rice, 194
Hopping John, 194
Lemon Dill Rice, 197
Paella, 198
Paella Rice Mix, 198
Quick Red Beans and Rice, 195
"Some Like It Hot" Pepper Rice, 196
Spanish Rice, 196
Vegetable Rice, 197
Venetian Rice and Peas, 195
Roast Duck with Chambord and Grand
   Mariner, 143
Roast Pheasant with Brandy and
   Cream, 142

Roast Wild Duck, 145
Roasted Sweet Peppers, 238
ROLLS
Grandmother Spitz's Refrigerator
Rolls, 74
Parker House Rolls, 73
Sausage Rolls, 75
Romanof Beef Noodle Casserole, 193
Rosemary Lemonade, 39

S

SALADS
3 Bean Salad, 61
Apricot-Pineapple Salad, 57
Blue Crab Salad, 60
Cauliflower Salad, 61
Congealed Cranberry-Sour Cream
Salad, 58
Curried Shrimp and Rice Salad, 56
Dilled Tuna Salad, 60
Eggplant Aubergine Salad, 56
Fruit Bowl, 62
Fruit Slaw, 63
Herbed White Bean Salad, 62
Ice Box Slaw, 64
Layered Spinach Salad, 64
Shimmering Winter Salad, 58
Strawberry Pecan Congealed Salad,
59
Western Chicken Salad, 59
Salmon Loaf with Cucumber Sauce, 161
Sand Tarts, 277
Sassy Spaghetti, 182
SAUCE
Cocktail Sauce, 236
Cream Sauce, 237
Easy Barbecue Sauce, 236
Tartar Sauce, 237
Sauerkraut Relish, 233
Sausage Rolls, 75
Sausage-Vegetable Dinner, 116
Sauteed Shrimp, 153
Scalloped Pineapple, 243
Scalloped Potatoes and Ham, 116

Scotch-A-Roos, 278
SEAFOOD
Baked Flounder, 159
Baked Red Snapper, 164
Brazilian Shrimp and Cheese
Casserole, 156
Broiled Scallops, 152
Crab Imperial, 150
Florida Snapper with Green
Peppercorn Sauce, 163
Flounder Ambassador, 160
Ginger Steamed Bass, 149
Grouper Fillets, 159
Hunter's Bluefish with Horseradish
Sauce, 158
Marinated Tuna Steaks, 165
Overnight Salmon Strata, 162
Oyster Bake, 151
Salmon Loaf with Cucumber Sauce,
161
Sauteed Shrimp, 153
Seviche, 153
Shrimp Creole, 154
Shrimp Etouffee, 155
Shrimp Newburg, 150
Stacey's Low Country Boil, 157
Seafood Fettuccine, 190
Seafood Lasagna, 191
Seafood Quiche with Rice Crust, 93
Secret Ribs, 104
Seminole Crackers, 24
Sensational Double Layer Pumpkin Pie,
292
Seviche, 153
Shimmering Winter Salad, 58
Shrimp and Scallops Pasta, 188
Shrimp Creole, 154
Shrimp Etouffee, 155
Shrimp Newburg, 150
"Skinny" Dip for Vegetables or
Crackers, 21
Smoked Wild Duck, 145
So Good Leftover Turkey, 135
"Some Like It Hot" Pepper Rice, 196
Sopa Seca de Fideo, 181

SOUPS
Black Bean Soup, 55
Brie Soup, 48
Broccoli Soup, 51
Chicken and Pasta Stew, 48
Chili #1: Hot and Spicy, 45
Chili #2: Meatless Chili, 46
Cold Peach Soup with Blueberries, 43
Hot and Sour Soup, 49
Lentil Soup, 54
Mother's Cucumber Soup, 44
Old Fashion Beef Stew, 53
Piccadillo (Spanish Stew), 47
Potato Soup with Rivels, 50
Pumpkin Soup, 52
Sour Cream Biscuits, 70
Sour Cream Coffee Cake, 250
Spaghetti Reina, 182
Spanish Rice, 196
Spiced Blueberries, 239
Spiced Peaches, 242
Spicy Baked Beans, 205
Spicy Leg of Lamb, 109
Spicy Lentil Spaghetti, 177
Spicy Meatballs, 28
Spicy Pork Roast, 113
Spinach Balls, 25
Spinach Casserole, 221
Spinach Dip, 22
Spinach Pate, 33
Squash-Tomato Casserole, 221
Stacey's Low Country Boil, 157
Steak Marinade, 234
Strawberry Cake, 259
Strawberry Nut Bread, 80
Strawberry Pecan Congealed Salad, 59
Stuffed Potatoes with Crab Meat, 218
Stuffed Shells Florentine, 175
Stuffed Zucchini, 224
STUFFING
Black Bean Stuffing, 229
Corn Stuffing, 230
Wild Rice Stuffing, 230
Sugarless Apple Pie, 286
Sun-dried Tomato Spaghetti Sauce, 181

Sweet and Sour Asparagus, 203
Sweet Potato Molasses Pie, 291
Sweet-and-Sour Pork Chops, 111
Swiss Steak, 104

T

Tahini (Sesame Paste Dip), 17
Tartar Sauce, 237
Teriyaki Chicken Wings, 30
Tiger Catnip, 26
Toast Points, 33
Toffee, 268
Tortellini with Dill Pesto, 174
Tri Stuffed Celery, 32
Turkey Basting Marinade, 234
Turkey Lasagna, 186
Turkey Tetrazzini, 187

V

Vegetable Dip, 22
Vegetable Lasagna, 180
Vegetable Mix-Up, 226
Vegetable Rice, 197
Vegetable Turkey Pie, 134
VEGETABLES
Apricot-Glazed Sweet Potatoes, 220
Artichoke Hearts with Spinach, 202
Artichokes with Avgolemono Sauce, 201
Asparagus Casserole, 203
Baked Lima Beans, 207
Broccoli Casserole, 208
Broccoli with Lemon Sauce, 208
Brussels Sprouts Almandine, 209
Calico Beans, 204
Carrot Fritters, 212
Carrots Au Gratin, 212
Corn Casserole, 213
Corn Fritters, 213
Creamed Cabbage with Walnuts, 211
Crispy Potato Wedges, 219
Deviled Tomatoes, 225
Ford-Hook Lima Beans Plus, 206

Fried Green Pepper Rings, 217
Fried Green Tomatoes, 225
Green Beans India, 206
Green Beans with Herbs, 205
Mrs. Correli's Eggplant Casserole,
    214
Mushroom Strudel, 215
Orange Beets, 207
Parmesan Eggplant with Yogurt,
    214
Peas with Mint, 217
Potato Casserole, 216
Red Cabbage and Apples, 210
Spicy Baked Beans, 205
Spinach Casserole, 221
Squash-Tomato Casserole, 221
Stuffed Potatoes with Crab Meat,
    218
Stuffed Zucchini, 224
Sweet and Sour Asparagus, 203
Vegetable Mix-Up, 226
Vidalia Onion Casserole, 216
Zucchini "Don't Even Know it's a
    Veggie" Casserole, 223
Zucchini with Almonds, 222
VEGETARIAN
Black Bean Burritos, 166
Chili Relleno Casserole, 165
Fried Tofu, 169
Gardener's Pizza, 168
Italian Spaghetti and Pecan Balls,
    167
Zucchini Pie, 170
Venetian Rice and Peas, 195
Venison Curry, 139
Venison or Elk Stew, 140
Venison Ragout, 137
Venison Scallopini, 138
Venison Steak, 136
Vidalia Onion Casserole, 216
Vidalia Onion Dip, 21
Virginia Buttermilk Biscuits, 72
Virginia Settler's Punch, 34

W

Waffles, 67
Waikiki Meatballs, 98
Wassail, 38
Western Chicken Salad, 59
Wild Goose, 147
Wild Rice and Mushroom Quiche, 92
Wild Rice Stuffing, 230
Williams Triffle, 263

Z

Zucchini Bread, 76
Zucchini "Don't Even Know it's a
    Veggie" Casserole, 223
Zucchini Pie, 170
Zucchini with Almonds, 222

UNDER THE CANOPY
GFWC Tallahassee Junior Woman's Club
P. O. Box 944
Tallahassee, Florida 32302
(904) 847-5158

Please send me _____ copies of UNDER THE CANOPY at $16.95 plus $3.00 shipping and handling per book. Florida residents add 7% sales tax.

Please make checks payable to:
        GFWC TALLAHASSEE JUNIOR WOMAN'S CLUB

Enclosed is my check or money order for $_____.

Name _____
                                    (print)
Address _____

City/State/Zip _____

Telephone (   ) _____

Please allow 6 to 8 weeks for delivery.

UNDER THE CANOPY
GFWC Tallahassee Junior Woman's Club
P. O. Box 944
Tallahassee, Florida 32302
(904) 847-5158

Please send me _____ copies of UNDER THE CANOPY at $16.95 plus $3.00 shipping and handling per book. Florida residents add 7% sales tax.

Please make checks payable to:
        GFWC TALLAHASSEE JUNIOR WOMAN'S CLUB

Enclosed is my check or money order for $_____.

Name _____
                                    (print)
Address _____

City/State/Zip _____

Telephone (   ) _____

Please allow 6 to 8 weeks for delivery.

🌳 UNDER THE CANOPY

Ship _____ gift copies to:

Name _____
                                        (print)

Address _____

City/State/Zip _____

Gift Card Message:

_____

_____

_____

🌳 UNDER THE CANOPY

Ship _____ gift copies to:

Name _____
                                        (print)

Address _____

City/State/Zip _____

Gift Card Message:

_____

_____

_____